Guest-edited by Maggie Toy and Charles Jencks

MILLENNIUM ARCHITECTURE

ACA

editor	Maggie Toy
managing editor	Helen Castle
production	Mariangela Palazzi-Williams
advertisement sales	Jackie Sibley - Tel: 01243 843272
design	Mario Bettella and Andrea Bettella / Artmedia
consultants	Catherine Cooke, Terry Farrell, Kenneth Frampton, Charles Jencks, Heinrich Klotz, Leon Krier, Robert Maxwell, Demetri Porphyrios, Kenneth Powell, Colin Rowe, Derek Walker

EDITORIAL OFFICES 4th Floor, International House
Ealing Broadway Centre, London, W5 5DB
Tel: 0181 326 3800 Fax: 0181 326 3801

SUBSCRIPTION OFFICES: John Wiley & Sons, Ltd
UK Journals Administration Department
1 Oldlands Way, Bognor Regis
West Sussex, PO22 9SA
Tel: 01243 843282 Fax: 01243 843232
e-mail: cs-journals@wiley.co.uk

USA AND CANADA John Wiley & Sons, Inc.
Journals Administration Department
605 Third Avenue, New York, NY 10158
Tel: + 1 212 850 6645 Fax: + 1 212 850 6021
cable jonwile telex: 12-7063
e-mail: subinfo@wiley.com

Photo Credits Abbreviated positions: b=bottom, c=centre, l=left, r=right, t=top.
Cover © David Lewis; p1 © Mario Bettella; p5 © Mario Bettella; p6 British Architectural Library, RIBA, London; p7 (tl) Guildhall Library, Corporation of London; p7 (tr, c&b) The Press Office, South Bank Centre, London; p9 © Charles Jencks; pp10-11 courtesy RSA Press Office; p12 & p13 (b) with thanks to Kieran Conry, Catholic Media Office; p13 EPA/PA News; p14 courtesy of the National Museum of Science and Industry; p16 NMEC/Hayes Davidson; p17 courtesy Stephen Bayley; p18 courtesy Pan Macmillan; p19 courtesy Fundacio Mies van der Rohe Barcelona, photos: Pau Maynes; p20 courtesy Michael Wilford and Partners, model photos: Richard Davies; p22 courtesy Daniel Libeskind, photos of model shots: © Sebastian Pfütze; pp24-25 dome show animation stills: courtesy Mark Fisher Studio; p25 (t) and (cl) NMEC/Hayes Davidson; p25 (cr) NMEC/SHAM; p25 (b) NMEC; p27 © Grant Smith/Richard Rogers Partnership/NMEC; p28 (b) and p29, © Mario Bettella; pp30, 32 and 33 courtesy Zaha M Hadid; p34-35 NMEC/Hayes Davidson; pp34 drawing courtesy Eva Jiricna Architects; p36 (t) photo of topping out of zone: NMEC/Mark Power/ Network; pp36-37 photos: courtesy Eva Jiricna Architects; p38(tl) courtesy Future Systems; p38 (c) courtesy the Design Council; p38(tr); p39 (c) and p39 (br) courtesy Expo 01, photos Yves Andre; p38(br) © Charles Jencks; p39(b) courtesy Hunt Thompson Associates; p40 photos: Andrew Putler; p43 courtesy Future Systems, photos of models: Richard Davies; p43 courtesy Future Systems, images and detail of roof modules: FS/Hayes Davidson; p44 (t) © Dennis Gilbert, View; p44 (b) courtesy Alsop & Störmer, © Richard Coyne; p45 copyright: Dennis Gilbert, View; pp46-47 courtesy Nicholas Grimshaw & Partners, photos: Imagination; p48 courtesy Hunt Thompson Associates; p49 (t) and (c) courtesy Edward Cullinan Architects; p49(b) courtesy Andrew Wright Associates; pp50-51 courtesy Hunt Thompson Associates; pp52-57 photos: © Charles Jencks; p58 (t) © AHMM, Studio Myerscough, British Council and Design Council; p58 (b) courtesy the Design Council; p60 (t) (b) photos: EPA/PA News; p60 (c) courtesy Israel Ministry of Tourism; p63 (t) & (b): © Barthélémy Ruggeri/Mairie de Paris; p63 (b) © Spanish National Tourist Office, London; pp62-63 EXPO 01, photos: Yves Andre; pp66-69 courtesy Expo 2000 Hannover; pp70-71 courtesy Hennin, Normier, Lelièvre; pp72-73 courtesy the Olympic Co-ordination Authority, photos: Bob Peters, Highlight Studios; p75 (t) & (b) © Edwin Heathcote; p77 (l) © Edwin Heathcote; p78 courtesy Richard Meier & Partners; p79 © Jock Pottle/Esto; pp80-81 courtesy Rafael Moneo Architect; p82 (b) and (t) courtesy Renzo Piano Workshop, p82 (b) photo: © G Berengo Gardin; p83 sketches: courtesy Renzo Piano Building Workshop; p83 (b) copyright: Publiton; p84 sketches: courtesy Renzo Piano Building Workshop; p84 photo: G Berengo Gardin; p85 sketches: courtesy Renzo Piano Building Workshop; p86-94 © Charles Jencks; p96-98 (t) courtesy of the V&A Picture Library; p98 (b) courtesy Solid State Industries Ltd; p99 courtesy Ron Arad Associates; p100 courtesy of Frédéric Borel; p101 courtesy of Frédéric Borel; p102 (t) courtesy of Frédéric Borel; p102 (c) courtesy of Christian de Protzamparc, © Nicolas Borel; p102 (b) courtesy of Grumbach and Didier Gallard, photos: Martine Cornier; p104 photos: © Iain Borden; p105 portrait of LOT/EK: Danny Bright; p106-108 photos: © Paul Warchol; p112 drawing courtesy David Chipperfield Architects; p112 photo by Jaap Oepkes, courtesy of the River and Rowing Museum.

First published in Great Britain by Academy Editions
a division of
JOHN WILEY & SONS
Baffins Lane, Chichester, West Sussex PO19 1UD

ISBN 0-471-72024-0
ISSN 0003-8504

Architectural Design vol 69 11-12/1999 Profile 142

ANNUAL SUBSCRIPTION RATES 2000: UK £135.00 (institutional rate), £90.00 (personal rate), £60 (student rate); Outside UK US$225.00 (institutional rate), $145.00 (personal rate), $105 (student rate). AD is published six times a year. Prices are for six issues and include postage and handling charges. Periodicals postage paid at Jamaica, NY 11431. Air freight and mailing in the USA by Publications Expediting Services Inc, 200 Meacham Ave, Elmont, Long Island, NY 11003.

SINGLE ISSUES: UK £19.99; Outside UK $32.50. Order two or more titles and postage is free. For orders of one title please add £2.00/$5.00. To receive order by air please add £5.50/$10.00.

All prices are subject to change without notice.

POSTMASTER: send address changes to AD, c/o Publications Expediting Services Inc, 200 Meacham Ave, Elmont, Long Island, NY 11003.

Printed in Italy

contents

CHARLES JENCKS
INTRODUCTION – MILLENNIUM TIME-BOMB

The Christian calendar and the idea of time, as a creative event with a beginning, middle and end, have conditioned world history to a degree no one could have expected. The year 1000 was celebrated in the West, and looked at differently from all other years. In 1971 I wrote a book, *Architecture 2000, Predictions and Methods,* which made a prediction about which I was sure: that the year 2000 would be different from any other year. Because so many people invested in the idea, it *had* to be unique. I called this a good example of the Oedipus Effect, and I was confident of being right: as with Oedipus, a prediction was bound to influence the predicted event.

Since 1790, and the book *L'An Deux-Mille*, the countdown, and Oedipus Effect, gathered strength. This grew through the 19th century to reach one high point with Edward Bellamy's *Looking Backward, 2000–1887* and then, in the early 20th, it reached another crescendo – with the Futurists' *New City for Milan 2000*. Interest waned until the 1960s and the Kennedy era, when optimism about the future, and multinational planning for future markets, sparked another round of 2000ism. American commissions called the year 2000 brainstormed the possible scenarios, French and Japanese think-tanks laid out the likely *futuribles* (as opposed to the Futurists, they stressed plural pathways as the only intelligent method of prediction). *The Sunday Times,* even *AD*, had 2000 features. Since the 1960s many corporations have caught the millennial fever, partly because big business must think far ahead and partly because the three big zeroes concentrate the mind like an ultimate deadline, and the hope of hitting three lemons on a fruit machine. For reasons we will mention, Britain invested more in the Millennium than any other country – Germany, America, Japan, Italy – probably all of them combined.

Well, in the obvious way I was right: Oedipus had his usual tragic revenge and the Millennium year is completely different from any other, but in another way I missed the point. Like Tony Blair launching the Dome in February 1998 – WHY THE DOME IS GOOD FOR BRITAIN – I forgot, completely, to mention Christ and the fact that it is Christian eschatology that sets the tune. Whether one likes it or not, and 95 per cent of the world do not believe in biblical description and forecast, the year 2000 celebrations carry an undeniable Christian content. Most of the predictions and the books I have mentioned, did not recognise this fact and even Christians have been slow to realise the time-bomb ticking away in the world's calendar; but it is irrefutable, not to be escaped.

As the reader will find, it has made inevitable the question: 'Celebrations – sacred or secular?' The year 2000 forces us to look at the basic questions – where we have come from and who we are now – not because we want to look, but because that date is culturally and politically loaded, to a degree greater than 1492, 1789 and 1968. We have to ask, 'What is being built for these celebrations and since so much money is being spent, what do they mean?' They show, I think, we have clearly moved into a new era, the Post-Christian period, with a content that celebrates science, the earth, ecology and Neo-Enlightenment values. What this means, positively and sadly, is the subject of the last essay.

There is another basic question which the anniversary forces on us. If one is going to make a spectacle and spend a fortune celebrating a date, how well is that money used, how well have the architects performed? No doubt, in Britain, some of the best architects have got the plum commissions: Foster, Rogers, Hopkins more than one each; Grimshaw and Farrell some very big ones; and good, lesser-known architects have also been given a chance. The question critics raise here and partly answer is: Are these architects performing at their best, most creative; or are they producing watered-down, safe versions of their previous work? Have they risen to the occasion, challenged society, or produced risk-free architecture? And, if it is the latter, who is to blame? Society, which sets impossible deadlines and strangles architects with budgets and lawsuits; or the government that does not give a clear lead; or commercial clients who demand formulaic solutions; or those who dream up the content, those focus groups and Imagineers, ex-Disney? As Stephen Bayley and others point out, the Millennium shows we are moving into a focus-group culture, where leaders wait for a committee, or supposedly representative group, to decide policy. Whatever virtues this may have as democratic action, its cultural results are not far from architecture by committee.

The other looming issue concerns the Christians themselves. It is really their symbolism and calendar – how well have they led us into the next 1000 years? Were they, any more than secular society, prepared for the media event? Thoughtful Christians, faced with the way commercial society hijacked the event, said it would be another case of worshipping the Golden Calf. Christians have enough domes, they do not need an expensive one funded by multinationals intent on advertising their wares. Better, as the Pope and Cardinal Hume said, to have a Jubilee, the forgiveness of debts, particularly those of the Third World, and better to celebrate the Christian virtues of humility, charity and love. Behind the scenes since 1998, however, a tawdry scene of intrigue was occurring within the Establishment. The question at issue was whether the Archbishop of Canterbury would be allowed a 30-second, possibly one-minute, prayer, minutes before 11:59, 1999. The BBC, which has rights to broadcast this world event, said, in effect 'No, too boring, viewers will turn off'; the NMEC (New Millennium Experience Company) thought it might conflict with the happy mood of good cheer; the Queen said, 'Yes, we must pray'. That too was Cardinal Basil Hume's much quoted dying wish, quickly brought into the debate – and finally the wish of Blair and Hague.

'The battle of the one-minute prayer' which every week produced an official 'yes' and 'no', showed, if nothing else, that we do live in a Post-Christian culture. But the real question is: What do we do, for the next 1000 years, with that shift in culture? What does it mean? This is the main question we have faced, if not answered, in this issue.

Millennium Dome, view from west

PETER MURRAY
1851 AND ALL THAT

Interior of the Crystal Palace, looking north

In terms of national celebrations, the Millennium Dome has had plenty of precedents – the Festival of Britain, the British Empire Exhibition and the Great Exhibition. Here Peter Murray takes a brief look at some of the Dome's predecessors to see what it has to live up to.

When the Prime Minister launched the New Millennium Experience at a press conference in February 1998 he described the 'long and hard' Cabinet discussion as to whether to go ahead with the Dome. 'One of the clinching arguments for me' he said, 'came when John Prescott [Deputy Prime Minister] and Jack Straw [Home Secretary] talked about their memories, deep and personal, of the Festival of Britain.'

'I want today's children to take from it an experience so powerful and memories so strong that it gives them that abiding sense of purpose and unity that stays with them through the rest of their lives.'

The Festival of Britain of 1951 will be a hard act to follow. It took place just six years after the war; rationing was still in place and life was generally drab and grey. The festival provided an image of regeneration, of hope and belief in the future. The idea was mooted in 1945 by the editor of the *News Chronicle*, Gerald Barry, for a great trade and cultural exhibition in 1951 which would proclaim Britain's recovery from the war. The government wanted to pare this down to a trade exhibition accompanied by an art show. However, with the appointment of Herbert Morrison as 'Lord Festival' and Gerald Barry as Director General a wider sense of fun and enthusiasm was injected into the enterprise.

While some might carp at the bastardised Modernism promulgated by the festival, there is no doubt that it had a deep and lasting effect on Britain's attitude to progress and design. It created a new confidence that lived up to its soubriquet as a 'tonic for the nation'. It therefore had much in common with the British Empire Exhibition held at Wembley in 1924 – six years after the end of the Great War. At its opening King George V declared 'the British Empire Exhibition open and I pray that by the blessing of God it may conduce to the unity and prosperity of all my people and to the peace and wellbeing of the world'.

In 1924 the area around the Wembley exhibition was open parkland so that visitors could experience 'all the charm of a gracious bit of English countryside'. The architecture favoured the Neo-Classical although the recent discovery of Tutankhamen's tomb led to a shift in the application of decorative motifs. Each of the dominions, India and the colonies displayed products and manufactured goods, arts and crafts, history and culture. The exhibition's aims were to stimulate trade, 'strengthen the bonds that bind the Mother Country to her sister states and daughter nations, to bring all into closer touch with one another, to enable all who owe allegiance to the British flag to meet on common ground, and to learn to know each other. It is a family party, to

which every part of the Empire is invited, and at which every part of the Empire is represented.'

While the intention of the exhibition was to spearhead a revival in Britain's trade and industrial growth, history was not on its side. Western Europe and North America were leading the way in new technologies. The Empire, having had to develop and adapt its own resources during the war, was not the market for Britain's goods it once was. Indeed, one of the main effects of the exhibition was the establishment of Australia as a major exporter to Britain of dairy produce.

The great 'White City' Franco-British Exhibition of 1908 was successful both as a trade event and as a public spectacle. As part of the entente cordiale of Edward VII's reign, the show owed much to the Chicago World Fair of 1905 for its architectural style. Highly decorated palaces were set in grand gardens and lakes designed under the guidance of John Belcher (past president of the RIBA), and the Frenchman Marius Toudoire. The site was used for exhibitions until 1937 and today is being transformed into a major shopping centre designed by Ian Ritchie.

The Great Exhibition of 1851 was proclaimed by Prince Albert as the 'great exhibition of the industries of all nations'. It concentrated on British industries, with 50 per cent of the 100,000 exhibits from the British Empire. It was visited by 6 million people. Its influence today rests largely on the designs by Joseph Paxton for the Crystal Palace, which housed the main exhibition and provides a continuing inspiration to architects and engineers with an interest in new building technology, and in the permanent museums that remain on the South Kensington site.

Today, the Millennium Lottery projects will create a lasting memorial of 2000 for future generations, but will the Dome be remembered as long as the Crystal Palace? The contents of the Dome study subjects like religion, nationality, locality and the body – a philosophical approach that contrasts with the trade shows of 1851, 1908 and 1924. How well it interprets these only time will tell, although Tony Blair's comment that it should be 'exhilarating like Disney World and emotional and uplifting like a West End musical' does not suggest it will be taking the high ground.

Festival of Britain 1951 – site under construction

Postcard of the British Empire Exhibition, Wembley 1924

Royal Festival Hall by
night 1957

Skylon at the festival
of Britain by night

CHARLES JENCKS

AN IDEA BIG ENOUGH FOR A DOME

Only a month after Tony Blair publicly backed the plans for the Millennium Dome in his speech 'Why the Dome is Good for Britain', on 24 February 1998 at the Royal Festival Hall in London, an Academy Forum met at the Royal Academy of Arts to debate architecture and the Millennium. The crux of the discussion was the question of the Dome's programme. What was to be its big idea or driving force? This not only shed light on the search for meaning in architecture per se, but also sought questions about the direction that we are moving in on the brink of a new millennium. Charles Jencks, who chaired the debate, not only articulated the central concerns, but also proposed an alternative narrative for a new era. Though he circulated his ideas to Millennium organisers Jennie Page, Simon Jenkins, Stephen Bayley and others, he failed to gain a response.

In spite of two years of creative brainstorming, countless public surveys and the prospect of spending £758 million, the Dome still awaits its big idea. Ted Hughes outlined in *The Times* one interesting idea which might unite the 14 different zones, or themes, of the Dome into one plot: a millennial theatre of the mind. His proposal not only unifies a potpourri of activities, but it results in a shape that resembles a dome: the brain. In the end, however, this would be a problem, just one more abstract fragment of our life added to the other 14.

Can we really relate to, or get excited by, neuronal circuitry and the few specialised areas inside our cranium? I think the addition of sexual organs to the (presently) neutered body of the giant man/woman would give at least as much excitement and be almost as relevant since it is an open question whether sexuality or brainpower has counted for more in terms of evolutionary success. Having two sexes has not only spurred growth of the brain and provided infinite pleasures but, for the last billion years, has multiplied the powers of DNA to resist degradation. As the main cosmic protagonist, sex is hard to beat.

Those who are critical of the whole millennial celebration have a point. If one is going to spend £4 billion or £5 billion welcoming in the year 2000, then there ought to be an idea that is at least as strong as the one which ushered in the year 1000. Christians have rightly protested at the banality of content though they have been late to offer countersuggestions. Even the Pope, who is set to celebrate the event on Mount Sinai like Moses II, as he is known among Italian prelates in Rome, remains tied to a backwards looking view of the future. Furthermore, as a global event, the Millennium has to address all religions, and a good deal of paganism and atheism as well, so the content cannot be contained within a Christian story.

A delicate question: Is there a coherent narrative which can acknowledge the contribution of Christianity to forming a world culture that also takes into account the new view of the universe and our place in it? Put another way: Is there a story, equivalent to that told in the Old and New Testaments, which can act as a guide for the next 2000 years? Another rhetorical question. Is there a story that partly grows out of the Genesis myth, appropriate to the Millennium, yet which acknowledges the truth that most of us now, in the West at any rate, are Post-Christians? The answer to each question, you won't be surprised, is 'yes'.

Cosmogenesis, the story of the universe from its origin some 15 billion years ago, is the new narrative, a gospel and drama only awaiting its James Joyce (or Eisenstein). Actually it has grown out of the Christian emphasis on linear time and it has the great advantage of being full of twists in the plot, all-encompassing and true. Although it has been told only partially, by scientists and such theologians as Thomas Berry (co-author with Brian Swimme of *The Universe Story*) it is emerging as the grand narrative which can unite every culture, every discipline and all the sciences in a magisterial sweep. Several millennial projects, such as Dynamic Earth in Edinburgh, are telling the story, but without anything that might be mistaken for art. What is the plot, and how could it pull together the 14 areas now under design for the Dome?

At its most basic it is a story, like that in Genesis, leading from simple cosmic beginnings of light, darkness and pure energy to a universe of complexity, richness and meaning. It is an account of jumps in organisation and, like several biblical events, a nasty and tragic story of catastrophes and mass extinctions. It is also a narrative of surprising emergence, of beauty and order coming out of chaos, of sentient creatures and cultures appearing almost instantly in cosmic time. There are missing chapters to this narrative, and some dispute over key issues such as whether progress is inevitable or contingent, but the basic outlines are now accepted around the globe and not only by scientists. Cosmogenesis, the idea of the universe as a single, creative, self-organising event has permeated every religion in contact with the West. Any culture tied into world trade and the Internet will absorb parts of this story through the media and the assumptions behind contemporary science. Ours is the first generation to be able to tell this history; it simply cannot be escaped.

Exhibition zones in the Dome already have absorbed elements of the narrative. The sections titled Atmosphere, Living Island and Shared Ground deal with the planet Earth, the environment and the British Isles. These could easily be extended to take in an account of the dramatic events of the first 11 billion years of cosmic history previous to the solar system. The way the universe emerged first as an explosive fireball of pure energy. Not quite a Big Bang – it was smaller than an electron and no one heard the explosion – the earliest era was a cosmic soup, or plasma of energy, which expanded miraculously fast and effectively. Here was the first miracle, and one much more extraordinary than those of ancient mythology: the universe, in its early inflationary period, expanded faster than the speed of light to balance the force of expansion and contraction precisely and delicately for the next 15 billion years. A trillionth of a degree of difference and the universe would have either collapsed, or flown apart, long ago. A narrow escape: we, or the universe rather, just made it. It is a miracle, which we have only begun to understand since the early 1980s, that ought to be celebrated at the centre of the Dome, in the light and sound spectacle to be designed by Mark Fisher and the musician Peter Gabriel.

As the universe expanded and cooled it underwent another series of jumps, or what are known as symmetry breaks. Matter, atoms, the 250 or so primary particles, froze out of the primeval unity. Without this and further breaks in symmetry nothing of interest would have emerged – stars, planets and the complex molecules that make up life. This part of the story could be told not only in the central son et lumière but in the zone 'Atmosphere', for where else did the oxygen, ozone and other life-sustaining elements come from if not from the explosion of stars, the supernovae, which seeded our solar system.

The third dramatic jump in cosmic evolution was that of matter into life, some three and a half billion years ago, a theme clearly suited to the two environmental zones of the Dome. The exact origin of life may remain a mystery for a long time, but we already know the main stages of its ascent: from bacteria to the first small cells, the units of life, and then, after another billion years, to sexuality and the first plants and animals, some 700 million years ago. With the advent of life, the miracle of cosmic evolution – its fine-tuned balance – was supplemented by new rules of evolution, not only Darwinian competition but also ecological interdependence. Both jumps in organisation occurred at once and they made the universe enormously more complex and interesting, a stage to be marked and celebrated as a spiritual event. To say this raises key issues of a Post-Christian culture, for what is an appropriate response to the story of the universe? Is the account meaningless because there is no final goal of cosmic evolution, or are all of the leaps in organisation sacred because they result in greater complexity?

The answers to this are implied, at least, in the next zones of the Dome, those dedicated to the world of work and leisure and those designed around the themes of the body, mind and spirit. The first three eras of cosmogenesis – energy, matter and life – lead to the fourth, the period when culture and consciousness develop together. Obviously one can recount cosmic evolution in finer detail and distinguish many more acts in the drama than the four I have sketched, but these are the main ones. They reveal a plot tending towards ever greater richness, sentience, consciousness and feeling, a seeming direction to the universe. Did it have to produce life, animals, culture and us? This, inevitably, is the big question to be faced at the second millennium if not answered finally. It appears to many scientists, and Post-Christian theologians, that the laws of the universe have a predisposition towards greater levels of organisation even if they do not include an exact blueprint for us. Chaos, indeterminism and the freedom they allow are real; so, if the 15-billion-year history could be rerun again and again, it might have different outcomes.

Yet culture and consciousness seem to be an inevitability after the previous stages of complexity have been reached, a conclusion which has some spiritual significance even for an atheist. If the story of the universe leads to this conclusion, and if it is told with drama and art, then it can provide not only the big idea for the Dome, but something more enjoyable as well, a metanarrative that relates us to the biggest thing around.

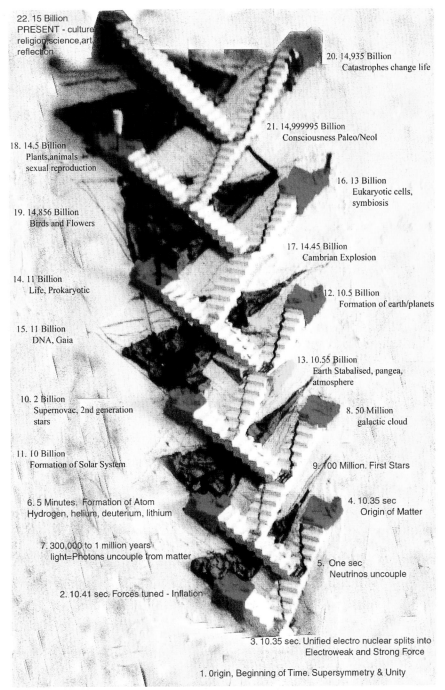

Charles Jencks, Universe Cascade, *the universe story in 22 jumps.*

* * *

Since 1990 I have worked with various scientists, artists and others on different models of the universe story: sculptural and landscape models that translate what we know of the cosmos into physical metaphors. The basic metaphor is that the universe develops not just as a gradual continuum, but in jumps. It is much more creative, dynamic, discontinuous and emergent than either the Christians or the Modernists could possibly conceive. We need new visual metaphors to reinterpret the story that is coming from contemporary discoveries; the old ones, such as Big Bang, are inadequate. We need a new poetics and aesthetics, at least as powerful as those of the past, that not only explain the new universe story, as do some Millennium projects, but make it sensually present; that give it some grandeur, pathos and immediacy.

Ecce Homo *by British artist Mark Wallinger, Fourth Plinth, Trafalgar Square, London. The first in a series of three contemporary sculptures organised by the Royal Society of Arts to be displayed in succession in Trafalgar Square until May 2001. In this statue, Wallinger was keen to emphasise the ordinary, everyday qualities of Christ.*

CLIFFORD LONGLEY
STAYING OUT OF THE MILLENNIUM DOME

Here Clifford Longley, a columnist for The Daily Telegraph *and a regular contributor to the Catholic international weekly* The Tablet, *probes the programme of the Millennium Dome and questions what form of national reflection should be taking place in the year 2000. Should we be emphasising only what we are doing right or be participating in a more effective soul-searching that will enable us to start moving forward in the right direction?*

What the official Millennium celebrations centred on the Greenwich Dome exhibit is not an insufficient desire to celebrate, nor an insufficiency of means for doing so, but an absence of any hint of humility or a modicum of modesty. If there is to be a time of national reflection, it is more important that we concentrate on what we are doing wrong than on what we are doing right. Frankly, politicians are in the business of pretending they are doing everything right, and they are therefore the last persons who ought to be in charge of events such as this one. Let us be upbeat by all means. But let us not be so upbeat as to be dishonest. As a nation we do not like overstatement. And as a nation, as Churchill once said of a colleague, we have a lot to be modest about.

Most people will be familiar by now with the so-called Jubilee 2000 campaign for the cancellation of Third World debt. For a while it seemed to have taken over from landmines as the most fashionable progressive international cause of the moment. But few people realise it was launched in 1994 by Pope John Paul II, from whom the term 'Jubilee' comes in this context. He invoked the Old Testament notion of a 'jubilee year' every 50 years – which is actually not half a 100, but seven times seven plus one.

That was the year when, among the Ancient Israelites, slaves were freed, debts between neighbours were cancelled, land returned to its original owners, quarrels were settled, and so on. From AD 1300 onwards, popes revived this idea, modifying it for their own purposes, and have conducted the celebration of these Jubilee years at regular intervals throughout the international Church ever since, though the custom was dropped on the Protestant side after the Reformation. Not surprisingly, perhaps, considering that it was all about indulgences.

Sometimes the Jubilee years were every half century, sometimes with mini-holy years after 25 years. These events are sometimes called Holy Years, and the present pope has proclaimed the year 2000 as the next one. Rome is Greenwich's most serious rival for the millennial accolade in the year 2000, with an estimated 30 million tourist visitors and pilgrims expected during the year. Last time I was in Rome, there did not seem to be a single public building or monument that wasn't covered in scaffolding as they cleaned and repaired it for the Millennium. As far as I know, all done without lottery money too. In that connection the Pope has set out on an ambitious, and some

would even say frankly incredible, programme of apologising to almost everyone the Roman Catholic Church might have upset over the last thousand years – women, Jews, Muslims, Protestants, whoever. This is also a debt-settling operation – moral debts, in this case. Not everyone has been satisfied with the apology, of course, but an apology is better than a curse. One recent part of that programme was the public 'profession of sorrow' at the Christian involvement in anti-Semitism in the past, which the Vatican issued in 1998. We may also expect apologies for the Crusades and the Inquisition and, long ago though these events may seem, many people do still feel bitter resentment over such things. And an apology, if sincere enough, is a good way of trying to ensure that the same things do not happen again.

Most of the other Churches have followed some or all of this Roman Catholic lead – certainly they are all behind the Jubilee campaign for the cancellation of Third World debt. They have had some success in persuading governments to acknowledge the need to do this. They also agree in seeing the Millennium as an essentially spiritual moment, a time for reflection and new beginnings based on an honest appraisal of the past, including contrition for past misdeeds where necessary. All this seems to me a much healthier and more spiritual way for the Christian Churches to mark the Millennium than by attempting to claim a bigger share of whatever razzmatazz is being organised at Greenwich. In fact the merit of the Jubilee idea is that it makes the year 2000 a *sui generis* occasion for Christian celebration, without having to argue about the exact year, or indeed time of year, of Christ's birth. Or its relevance. We are, so to speak, having our own party, for our own reasons.

By focusing on an idea like international debt relief, the campaign unifies rather than divides people of different persuasions and backgrounds. The element of sorrow for past wrongs,

no matter how clumsily executed, also seems to strike a good spiritual note. In a sense, cancelling international debt is itself a form of repentance, for it recognises that many of the reasons why Third World countries got into debt in the first place are to do with their being exploited by the developed world. This applies especially to those countries that were ruthlessly used as pawns in the Cold War.

It is precisely the triumphalist tone of the British millennial celebrations that turns many people off them. How about a little repentance first? How about, for instance, the architectural profession asking itself who it has wronged these last 50 or 500 years, and seeking forgiveness? (And under architects, for these purposes, I would include 1960s town planners.)

But even worse, the triumphalism is essentially hollow. The Greenwich Dome, we are assured, is an occasion to celebrate all that is best about Britain. But who is to decide? Some 50 or 100 years ago there would be no difficulty – we had a ruling elite who could answer such questions for us, including a ruling cultural and artistic elite who would tell us what was good, and no arguing. And we also had, as a nation, a 'unifying idea' of ourselves. We were confident 50 or 100 years ago that our nation stood for a number of things which we could all agree on – it was a Christian nation, civilised, white, liberal, democratic, free and effortlessly superior to those elsewhere in the world to whom God had not dealt such a good hand. We quite rightly are not so sure about celebrating those things now, but what do we celebrate instead? Striking artificial postures we do not really believe in isn't going to impress anyone, not even ourselves.

The building of a Dome at great expense without telling us what is to go inside stands as a symbol of the bankruptcy of the basic postmodern idea. Post modernism as a cultural and philosophical force rather than an architectural style proclaims the ultimate reductionist idea, that there are no longer any meta-narratives, no truths or theories of humanity which are universally applicable or even universally meaningful. Your truth is as good as my truth is another way of saying there is no such thing as truth. So the 'big idea', as the year 2000 approaches, is that there

is no big idea. You build the Dome before you decide what to put into it. And you aren't even aware that there is a problem in what you are doing.

The Churches have been lobbying for a greater share and greater say in the Millennium process, but they have been doing so very half-heartedly and without much idea of what they really want. They send their troops into battle, but the staff officers behind the lines are full of misgivings.

Nobody in Christianity nowadays seriously maintains that Christ was born on 25 December of year zero AD, or perhaps it would be the back end of year minus one. It is just about true that without the birth of Christ in about 4 or 6 BC, plus grievous miscalculations of the calendar somewhere in the early centuries after his birth, the year which starts on 1 January next would not have had three noughts to it. So maybe there is a tenuous Christian claim to ownership. But we should not exaggerate. Some days of the week in English are named after pagan Nordic or Old English gods, and some months of the year after the gods of imperial Rome.

The Churches' real lack of enthusiasm for Greenwich – despite what they say up front – is partly because they are well aware that they cannot supply the missing Big Idea by themselves. Unconsciously, they might be nostalgic for a Christian past, but consciously they know that Britain is multicultural and multi-religious, and that the largest non-Christian religious idea in Britain, far larger than Christianity itself, is a confused spiritual agnosticism which answers a highly tentative 'Yes, on the whole', to the loaded question Gallop asked on one occasion without even knowing it was loaded: 'Do you, like most people, believe in nothing much these days?'

So the Churches have been pressing for a share of millennial funding and a share of Millennium Dome space largely out of a 'me too' instinct, a desire not to get left out if something important is happening. This posture demeans the Churches. They would earn far more credit if they stood aloof, and did their own thing in their own way. In fact there is no obligation on the Churches to succumb to Millennium fever at all. They don't get excited on

Castel Sant'Angelo, Rome.

Colonnade of St Peter's, Rome.

Pope John Paul II waving to a crowd of some 650,000 pilgrims gathered in Stary Sacz, Poland.

other New Year's Days. There would be dignity in sitting the Greenwich party out.

This 'me too' approach also obscures the fact that there is no agreed religious truth about British society, neither in the present day nor in the past. What happened at the Reformation, for instance? Was it a bottom-up rebellion against Church corruption – which used to be the received wisdom – or was it the imposition from above of an alien creed by the political powers-that-be, as revisionist historians of the period are now telling us? Was the Enlightenment our moment of rescue from superstitious dogma, or the moment we succumbed to the seductive but ultimately destructive notion that all things are susceptible to reason? How do you celebrate both those ideas at once?

Let us, at least for the sake of argument, agree that religion has made a vital contribution to British history and to the evolution of British identity. But exactly what was that contribution? Was it a contribution to repressive law and privileged order, or *laissez faire* economics, or social class structure, or even white racism? Or was it the foundation of the welfare state, the European Convention on Human Rights, and victory over Nazism in the Second World War?

Furthermore, any attempt to represent religion in exhibition form is bound to involve grievous misrepresentation. My guess is that it will make 'Christian Britain' seem even more archaic and remote from the present day, 'another country' where strange people did unusual things to themselves and each other. Churches which went along with that, in the hope of guaranteeing their presence under the Greenwich Dome, would be engaged in little short of self-mutilation.

This is by no means an anti-religious view on my part. I am simply concerned for religion's integrity. Nor should religious people boycott the proceedings. If the official celebrations can, whatever the difficulties, offer some meaningful salute to the human spirit – and I don't wish to sound too negative about the chances of them succeeding in that – then I shall be glad to be among those taking part and joining in. But what would appal me above all is the prospect of a 'Christian corner' somewhere in the Dome, a pathetic attempt to keep the flag flying in the midst of so much self-satisfied paganism. 'Spiritual gardens' are proposed – well, why not? The English have long liked to say that you can worship God in a garden – 'a lovesome thing, God wot,' indeed – as much as in a church (usually their excuse for not going near the latter). So let's have a garden or two, by all means. But let's not pretend it is some sort of Big Statement, except about gardening.

I recently asked a young acquaintance why people of his generation were taking to Gregorian plainchant so enthusiastically. Was this sudden fascination with the ancient music of the Western Church the beginnings of a religious revival? No; it was because, I was told, Gregorian chant was cool music to chill out to as one came down from taking Ecstasy at a party or disco. That seems to me the ultimate expression of postmodern cultural vacuity. I suspect that will be the role of so-called 'spirit level religion' in the Dome. (And can we now, please, finally and for ever dump that atrocious pun?) A good place to chill out in, perhaps, after the 'feel good' pandemonium elsewhere. Fine, if you like that sort of thing, I say in my best postmodern style, but don't let's confuse it with the real thing.

The above text is a revised version of a presentation given by Clifford Longley at the 'Look Forward in Anger: Debating Architecture and the Millennium' forum held in the Royal Academy of Arts, London, in March 1998.

Interior of St Peter's, Rome.

In contrast to the Millennium Dome, the Victorians had a clear idea what they wanted out of their exhibition. The profits of the 1851 Great Exhibition were great enough to purchase the land for the Science Museum (left), the Natural History Museum, the V&A, Imperial College and so on. One of the main movers behind the exhibition was Albert Prince Consort (above). The Christian certainty of the period meant that the exhibition was discussed in terms of technological and scientific progress and human advancement.

DAVID PAPINEAU

THE MILLENNIUM AS A MATTER OF CONTINGENCY

For David Papineau, Professor of Philosophy at King's College London, the programme of the Dome represented 'a failure of nerve'. At the 'Look Forward in Anger: Debating Architecture and the Millennium' forum, held at the Royal Academy of Arts in March 1998, he advocated a secular approach to the millennium which would confidently celebrate the advancement of human intelligence over the last 100,000 years.

The Millennium is an essentially contingent event. In fact it's contingent at least twice over. The first contingency is to do with the date: 1 January 2000. This date hasn't got any intrinsic significance; it's just an artefact of our calendar system. I know that some people would point out that it's 2000 years since the birth of Christ, but I don't think that should be taken to be of serious significance here – even if we leave to one side a number of awkward questions, like: 'Shouldn't that be 2001, because Christ's first year was the year 1? And shouldn't it be 25 December?' Even if we leave these questions to one side, there's the much more important fact that less than one-sixth of the British population thinks of the Millennium celebration as anything to do with the birth of Christ. It's not that they don't think the religious connection is important; they don't think about the religious connection at all. I must confess that I myself hadn't specially connected 2000 with the birth of Christ until I was asked to speak here today and realised that some people did. The irrelevance of religion doesn't mean that we haven't got a reason to celebrate something though. Even though I don't think of 2000 as anything to do with the birth of Christ, I, like everybody else, am aware that 2000 is coming up, that this is a big date, that it's something to mark. And the reason for celebration is just that our calendar system makes 2000 a time-mark, a big round number, something that most of us have been anticipating all our lives, precisely because it's a striking number in the system that all of us mark time by. I think it's rather like being a child, and watching the mileometer of the car getting up towards 999, and you're dying to see it turn over to 1000, and you look forward to it, and you're rather upset if you miss it. I feel like that about 2000. I've been waiting for it to turn over all my life, and I'll be rather upset if I miss that too.

So that's one contingency: we happen to have a striking date coming up soon. The other big contingency, of course, is the National Lottery. The Lottery means we have a lot of money to spend on a party to mark our time-mark. This differentiates Britain from most of the other countries in the world. They are all doing something or other to mark the beginning of the Millennium, but none of them seems to be getting into the Millennium business on the same scale as we are. And the reason, of course, is that they don't all have a new source of large amounts of, whatever we call it – public money, citizens' money, loose money – which is destined to be spent on luxuries rather than necessities. So these are two big contingencies, and if you add to them a few smaller ones, like the fact that the world counts time from Greenwich Mean Time, and that there is a lot of space at Greenwich to do something with, we end up with all the excuses we could need for a celebration.

That's why, even if the 'why' is just a matter of contingency, I think there is a good enough reason for a celebration. That leaves us with the question of 'what'? If we're going to celebrate, what are we going to celebrate? Here it gets trickier, because nobody seems to have any good answers to this question. The first thought, of course, is that we should be celebrating in some sort of religious or spiritual context. Fortunately, however, even though we have an established Church in this country, and a prime minister who's a practising Christian, we seem to have avoided that pitfall. We don't have to count numbers to see the obvious objection. Though it's not irrelevant that Britain has one of the lowest numbers of practising religionists in the world, the real trouble with the religious line is 'Whose religion?' In a multicultural, modern Britain, with a preponderance of devout atheists, to celebrate any particular religion, even Christianity, would only rule the majority out of the party.

Here's another idea: roughly, we should celebrate everything. That's 'everything' as in 'the theory of everything'. We should celebrate the whole history of the universe from the Big Bang onwards. The trouble with that, though, is that most of that history is nothing much to do with us. We weren't around when the Big Bang happened; nor were we around for most of the rest of the history of the cosmos. From the point of view of the cosmos we're just a blip, a lucky accident. A local happenstance. We're lucky to be here and not guaranteed to be around for ever. So I think if we're going to celebrate something it should be something to do with us, the human beings. It ought to be a celebration of human achievement. It ought to be a story of how the human intellect has enabled us to move in a brief 100,000 years or so from simple hunter-gatherers through ancient civilisations to the point where it's commonplace to be able to work your hugely powerful desktop computer from anywhere on the Earth's surface by manipulating a hand-held radiotelephone via a satellite .

What I have in mind here is not just the gee whiz, Flash Gordon aspect of technology; what I think is more important is the fact that humans have managed to figure out so much about the nature of the universe and our place in it with brains that weren't really made for that. It's been very hard work, given that our brains were originally designed to help us run around on the savannah, to work out as much as we have. Yet these simple brains have managed to figure out the underlying structure of matter, the key to the genetic code, and so much else, including the fact that our brains were designed for running around the savannah. And that really is an incredible achievement. If you want something to be proud of and celebrate, it's the obvious solution. Unfortunately, that doesn't seem to be much to do with

In contrast to our Victorian counterparts our organisation of the Dome seems to signal 'a bad failure of nerve'. Few of the zones in the Millennium Dome have any more than a tangenital relationship with human achievement.

what's actually going to happen inside the Dome. (The remarks that I'll be making from now on are to do with the Millennium Experience, the most visible aspect of the celebration, and clearly don't apply to the many other Millennium projects, many of which have their own rationale and justification and don't need any further celebration to justify them).

You might think from some of the formulae that have been published about the Millennium Experience that the planners have in mind something like the celebration of human intellectual achievement and science that I'm advocating. We're sometimes told that the Millennium Experience is going to celebrate: 'work, rest and play, bodies and minds, and the environment' and 'who we are, what we do, and where we live'. It's also meant to be about the future. Maybe that's supposed to be a celebration of human intellectual achievement. I don't know. But if that's what the planners did originally have in mind, and I guess it's not clear, something seems to have happened on the way to the Dome, because there seems to have been a bad failure of nerve. Perhaps the signs have been around for some time: trips to Disneyland and co-opting children to suggest installations. Those don't seem like the actions of a team who have a clear vision of what they're after. And I think that what we've seen so far only bears out these worries. Of the six zones announced so far, possibly two have something substantial, if tangential, to do with human achievement, and the rest simply look like funfair sideshows.

I'd like to finish by looking back to the Great Exhibition of 1851. The exhibition was a huge success and universally acclaimed. The profits ended up being large enough to buy the land on which we now have the Science Museum, the Natural History Museum, the V&A, Imperial College and so on. If you look back, this success wasn't an accident. The Victorians had a clear vision of what they were up to, and what they wanted to achieve. They wanted to celebrate human art and industry, and mark the level it had reached. One of the prime movers behind the scheme was Prince Albert, and he stated the vision very clearly. He wanted the exhibition to be 'a true test of the point of development at which mankind has arrived, a new starting point from which all nations would be able to direct their future exertions'. Of course there's a sense in which the Victorians had it easy. Their celebration of science and technological progress was set within the certainties of Christian religion, and for them this was what gave meaning to the advances of the human race. In 1851, if you think about it, Charles Darwin's bombshell was still eight years away, and had yet to start eating away at the edifice of religious belief. But while that's a real enough difference between us and the Victorians, I don't think this difference invalidates the comparison between the year 2000 and 1851. Nowadays we may know more and believe less, but we've still got just as much reason to celebrate the achievements of human science as they had. Of course we now know about the ills scientific advance can bring – over-population and pollution – but, come to think of it, the Victorians had pollution enough in their day. Maybe we now realise that the path to prosperity is not smooth, but it's foolish to infer from this that the achievements of science should be belittled. Even if science didn't in fact add a jot to our prosperity, the fact that we now know so much about the very big, the very small and the processes that give rise to species would be amazing enough. And of course science does add to prosperity. Even with all the downsides, I can't take seriously the idea that we'd be better off without science. If you do think that, just think about the infant mortality rate in 1851 and think about whether you'd really rather be back there.

Nowadays we know more and we believe less. Perhaps the believing less, perhaps the withering away of religion, means that we're left without anything, without a centre to be proud of. I would say that was a mistake too. After all, the certainties of religion aren't an unmixed blessing, as a brief glance around the globe will show you – Northern Ireland, the former Yugoslavia. If Britain is a secular society now, and I think it is, then that in itself is an achievement we can celebrate. Maybe some of you think that without religion everything falls apart, that we're left with nothing but a shell of superficial design and cheap entertainment. And maybe those responsible for the Dome feel that too. Certainly, it looks like that sometimes. If that's so, the Millennium is a lost opportunity, because I think we've got plenty of achievements to celebrate, if only we had the confidence to recognise them.

STEPHEN BAYLEY
FALLING OUT WITH THE DOME

As the creator of the Boilerhouse Project at the V&A in London and of the Design Museum, Stephen Bayley was an obvious choice for Creative Consultant of the Millennium Dome. After only six months in the job, however, he resigned amid considerable controversy. The experience became the starting point for Labour Camp *a humorous but informed account of the Blair government's obsession with style, image and novelty. At the March 1998 'Debating Architecture and the Millennium' forum, he explained why he felt the culture of management at the Dome was at odds with a creative spirit.*

My falling out with the Dome was not a falling out with the Dome as an idea. I'm 100 per cent enthusiastic about it. I think it's a splendid thing that a country like ours is making such a financial and spiritual, if you like, commitment to a major project like this. That's absolutely terrific. What I did find utterly incompatible with my own personal motivation – and I also feel to an extent I can represent the ideas and motivations of the architecture and design community, a community of professionals with which I'm pretty familiar – was that the style of management, the culture of management, of the whole project was entirely at odds with the creative spirit necessary to make this into an excellent project. Ultimately, of course, it's the politicians. By happy accident, just as I was scribbling these notes I came across a two-line poem by ee Cummings. Cummings wrote, 'A politician is an arse upon which everyone has sat except a man.' Now, when you have politicians – particularly politicians of a particular persuasion – mixed with civil servants (or at least people imbued with a public service mentality), I do think you have a special problem, particularly when you're trying to manage something as complex, as vigorous, as subtle and as full of communications potential as the Millennium Dome. I personally found that a great deal of the culture that existed actually inhibited creativity. I certainly don't want to be specific about individuals, still less about a professional caste, but a lot of the clichés about civil servants, I tend to find, are true. The whole culture with which the Millennium project is being organised does tend towards a furtive, neurotic secrecy. One of the first things, for instance, I wanted to do when I was there was to try and get a little bit of optimism, a little bit of joy and a little bit of enthusiasm into the organisation. I wanted to have a journalist attached to each of the 13 or so zones. I said, right, let's have a print or television or broadcast journalist of some sort working with each of these groups instead of this Kafkaesque business, the fortress mentality which pervades the whole Millennium Company. Everybody's bound by secrecy clauses. No one wants to talk to the press – the press are construed as enemies. That's a cumulative process. Every single thing that I found the Millennium Company dealing with was treated as a crisis rather than as an opportunity.

That's all in the past, but I do think there's a fundamental point about why I think the project is so muddled and heading for such mediocrity. It's this – it's back again to the public service mentality. The very thing that made British public servants so efficient at their jobs of running empires or running school dinners is exactly the same thing that prevents them from doing what is an executive task in what is an essentially creative business. That's to say that public servants are by training disallowed from reaching decisions, but in a project like this, particularly a project with a screaming obvious deadline, decisions are called for daily, yet no decisions were forthcoming.

Still, a great opportunity existed, I felt, to do something immensely worthwhile with the Dome at Greenwich, and of course there's a great tradition of events like this. One knows about 1851, Paris 1889, Paris 1925, New York 1938–9, the Festival of Britain 1951, even Montreal in 1967. These were great events which actually changed, in a way, history. The Great Exhibition of 1851 gave Britain symbolic ownership of industrial design just at the moment when manufacturing industry was becoming important; 1889 gave us the Eiffel Tower of course; 1900 announced Art Nouveau to the world; 1925 Art Deco and Le Corbusier. The Barcelona Pavilion, which Mies van der Rohe designed as a temporary exhibition in Barcelona in 1929, changed the whole pattern of the development of furniture and architecture in the 20th century. That, I think, is the sort of standard of content which should have been aimed for, and, I believe, was actually achievable. The very fact that the Dome is so enormous that Gustave Eiffel's tower could be laid on its side within it probably speaks volumes about the relative merits of 1889 and the year 2000. I strongly sense that all the money available should be spent on commissioning the very, very best architecture and design, not only from the extraordinary community of talent we have in this country but internationally too.

I also felt that sponsors shouldn't be treated cap-in-hand, please come to us and give us some money. I was with a German car company for most of today, and they said, 'What's all this Millennium stuff? We've just had a letter from somebody asking us for £12 million, and we don't know what it's all about.' That's not the way to do it. From all my experience of exhibitions – and all the ones I've been involved with have used sponsors – you get the sponsor to act as a partner and as a collaborator. You can persuade sponsors that the very popular public exhibitions – the exhibition we did in the Boilerhouse about Coca-Cola can claim to be one of the most popular in London in the postwar years; it rivalled Tutankhamen and the Impressionists in attendance – you can sell that sort of exhibition about popular culture to manufacturers. You can tell them, here's a fantastic opportunity to test-market for new products in a very perceptive clinic. The public is there. You can excite the public by showing them a vision of the future. Nothing sells exhibitions as much as a sense of voyeurism. You can also tell the public that there's an opportunity to

Stephen Bayley, Labour Camp, *Pan Macmillan (London)*, 1999.

participate; they can intercept the future. Manufacturers and architects can show them what they're thinking of in the future, and the public can actually intercept that future and have an influence on it. The sort of ideal I felt I should be aimed at was terribly, terribly simple. You should build the city of the future and the way you do it is to go to Sainsbury's and say, 'How would you like to test-market and idea for a new format inner-city store? I'm sure you'd love to. Twelve million perceptive people want to come and see it. Test-market that; test-market new produts. Please give us £6 million and we'll go and commission Frank Gehry or Santiago Calatrava, or somebody of similar stature and vision, to actually build it.' I thought the opportunity which existed in the Dome was to be the best, most imaginative and liberal client ever for the best ever architecture and design.

Even if the money had been spent on commissioning decent new street furniture, just that alone would have made it worthwhile. Instead, alas, what we've seen is a politically inspired slump towards vulgar mediocrity. I think this insults the public and short-changes history. Albert Einstein lectured at the New York World's Fair in 1939, and it didn't stop 14 million people attending that. Just today I've learnt that perhaps the most talented group of architects and designers working on the Dome have been unemployed – have been 'stood down', as they say in sporting circles – on the basis, and I paraphrase, that *Sun* readers would not understand what they are getting at. I think that's both insulting to the architects and designers and insulting to *Sun* readers. I think the truth is that the opportunity to do something great inside the Dome has not even been considered, let alone rejected. Mere ballsy rejection of excellence would have been one thing – that would have been stylish – but I don't believe excellence was ever really contemplated. Hence my famously glib, but I hope you found rather funny, remark about Peter Mandelson visiting Brixton, where he had seen voodoo sacrifice, and had it been proven to him that voodoo sacrifice would possibly win the next election, voodoo sacrifice he would indeed have had in the Dome. The whole lot has been judged on focus groups. As many of you here know, in the present government's last manifesto all the substantive words were tested on focus groups.

The point is that to make the Dome excellent it has to be driven by creative people prepared to step on toes, step on fingers – choose your own metaphor. Creative people by definition are unreasonable and risk-taking and enjoy thinking the unthinkable. Politicians, particularly the current batch of politicians, want safeness and predictability. I strongly believe that absolute excellence can most certainly be popular, but I don't believe that the slavish pursuit of mindless popularity is ever going to lead to excellence in architecture and design. I think what we saw when such contents as there were initially shown on 24 February

1998 showed that of such creativity as has been on display so far, the great majority is cliché and vapid kitsch. I think I just spluttered with despair when the large parent and child figure was shown us. I do strongly believe that the Millennium Dome will be judged ultimately on the artistic and intellectual quality of the contents, which I have to tell you is very low indeed. One-thirteenth of the interior of the Dome when I last saw it was devoted to a water ride where the visitors will sit on divan beds and listen to airport music. Call me an elitist if you like, but I simply don't think that's a worthwhile project for anybody's money. We also have dioramas of sunsets over the Serengeti. I'm serious!

I just remind you as well that the immense cost of this could have been spent on superb architecture and design, and stuff that genuinely changed the destiny of the nation. I think the cost of the magnificent Guggenheim Museum in Bilbao was about $100 million (£60 million), and I think that gives one very, very serious pause for thought.

There were a number of last straws in my six months' occupation with this fascinating project. The very last straw was Peter Mandelson's misjudged visit to Disney. I felt this was really, at its best, naive, I really don't think the Millennium Dome should be a theme park. I thought the naiveté was profound for the following reasons. First of all, Disney has been doing Disney since 1955 and has built up a peerless repertoire of technical expertise, and there would be no possibility, even if the time and budget existed, of imitating that. But I also felt why, when Marne La Vallée and Eurodisney are just three hours away from London, waste an opportunity by attempting a thin replica of Disney in Greenwich when there's a far better opportunity to do something original and challenging. Peter Mandelson and the others tend to dismiss critics like me as being professional cynics. I'm not at all; I'm enthusiastic about the idea of the project. Peter Mandelson would also say that all great public projects have their critics, and of course he's right, but I think there's an essential difference today. In 1851 and 1951 the philistines were on the outside criticising the organisers. I do think that today the philistines are on the inside.

The Millennium posed a great opportunity to produce buildings and objects that might change the course of contemporary design, such as the Barcelona Pavilion designed by Mies van der Rohe in 1929.

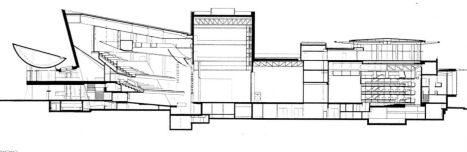

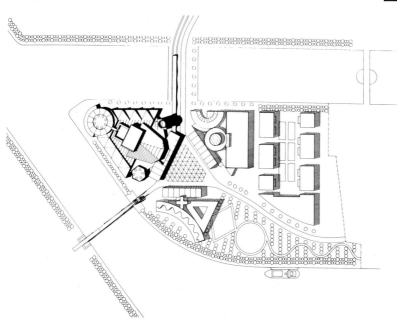

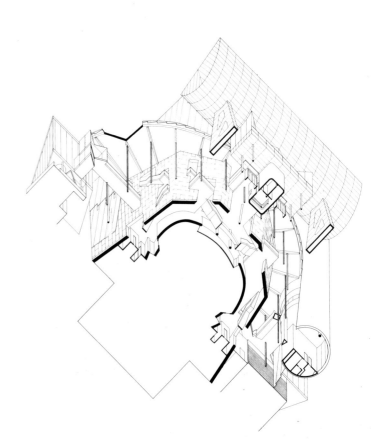

Michael Wilford and Partners, Lowry Centre, Salford: model shots (top); site plan and long sections through theatres (centre); and axonometric (bottom). The Lowry Centre is one of the 189 schemes supported by the Millennium Commission with National Lottery money.

SIMON JENKINS

A VERY PRIVATE VENTURE

THE TESTIMONY OF A MILLENNIUM COMMISSIONER

At the 'Look Forward in Anger' debate at the Royal Academy of Arts, in March 1998, Simon Jenkins, The Times columnist and Millennium Commissioner, gave an account from the inside of how the Millennium Dome came about and how it might be developing.

I thought it might be helpful if I went back over some of the history of Britain's Millennium celebrations. Projects like these are invariably treated with the sort of criticism in advance that this one has received it is helpful at least to bear that in mind, to see if there are other ways we can do it to avoid falling into the same pitfalls. We have studied 1951 in some detail – and in slightly less detail 1851 – and both exhibitions were regarded as unmitigated disasters before they opened. Both were greeted with far more severe criticism than the Dome before they opened. Both, from the moment they did open and the public saw what they were all about, were regarded as defining the morals of their age. It would be arrogant of us to think that we've got to the latter point yet, but then the Dome hasn't opened yet.

All of us involved in the project are now connoisseurs of the arts of British scepticism. We're also connoisseurs of the always difficult relationship between politics, in every sense of the word, and art and design, which at this stage are the major factors in this exhibition, this show, this experience. We're also connoisseurs of the famous 'schools and hospitals' argument, to which I shall also address one or two remarks.

The Millennium Commission was set up in 1994, and was asked to spend one-fifth of the Lottery money on celebrating the Millennium – that is really celebrating, not building schools and hospitals. Indeed, had we so wished, we would have been told, and you would all have agreed, that it would be quite wrong to spend money set aside by the Lottery on substituting for other forms of public expenditure. It was not meant for that. That was what we were told, and we couldn't do otherwise.

We also, if I may mildly correct a previous impression, were under the same restrictions as everybody else receiving the Lottery money: we could not initiate projects. Indeed, we were told that if we so much as breathed the initiation of a project we'd be guilty under the criminal law. We simply had to sit there and say whether whatever application we received through the front door was one to which we felt we could give the money. We had to be extremely general in the range of instructions or guidance that we gave potential applicants as to what might be acceptable. We decided – it was not unanimous but was hotly debated – that we would do more than just back projects up and down the country. We would do something specific to celebrate the year 2000. We discussed what and how much. Should it be a huge party? Should we put on a trade fair? Should we have a single exhibition or lots of exhibitions? I think rightly we took the view, which I felt very strongly, that with the money that we'd been

given for this purpose we should do one big show, not splurging the money around in lots of small shows. Could we really not repeat 1851 and 1951? We took a deep breath and said, yes.

We also had to decide how much of our money we would give. Arbitrarily, we said one-fifth. This whole game appears to go in fifths. Two hundred million of our money would go on this project and not a penny more. This was subsequently expanded by another £250 million of contingency money from future Lottery stream, but not from 'our money', and therefore not at the expense of any other projects during the gestation of the Dome experience. There is no substitution effect at all for the Dome from any other project funded by the Lottery from the moment that we'd taken that decision in 1994. I cannot emphasise that too strongly, because we're now accused of doing everything from closing down the Royal Greenwich Observatory in Cambridge to shutting down the Greenwich Theatre. They were not our business, sad though those closures might be.

The problem we then had was that we were not allowed to set up our own exhibition. In effect we were told that this had to be a private venture. That was the first eruption of politics into our project. We had to go out to the world and say, please come forward with a proposal for the celebration of the year 2000, and we then had, on the basis of competition, to judge which one of those proposals was best. I thought at the time, and I still think, that this was a flawed idea. However, it was required of us and we did it with the greatest expedition we possibly could. It is fair to say that we did lose time testing to destruction the theory that you could have a privatised exhibition in the year 2000. However, we learned a lot from it, so no time in that sense was wasted. It wasn't until the end of 1995 – which even so was only 18 months after the first idea – that we formulated the two-stage competition. This gave us the site of Greenwich and the Circle of Time that had originally been proposed by Imagination for Birmingham. We deliberately structured it that way, so that we could mix and match: we put the Circle of Time at Greenwich. We then had to see if the private sector would back it. The private sector wouldn't. We spent 1996 getting ourselves to the stage where we could put together a public sector company in time to give you something by the year 2000. I repeat that it was not necessarily time that was wasted, but it was time that was being spent, possibly unnecessarily, testing out the remit we had been given by statute, not by our own design.

In December 1996, a critical date that is engraved on my heart, we still didn't know if the next government would back the Dome. We had to let steel contracts in January, before the general election. We were then faced with what might have been the second eruption of politics into our project. We had the prospects of a new government coming into power in May of 1997 which might not back the project. Labour at the time said it was keeping an open mind on the project. We had to say to them, please back it now. We've got to let steel contracts, and we've got to hire staff.

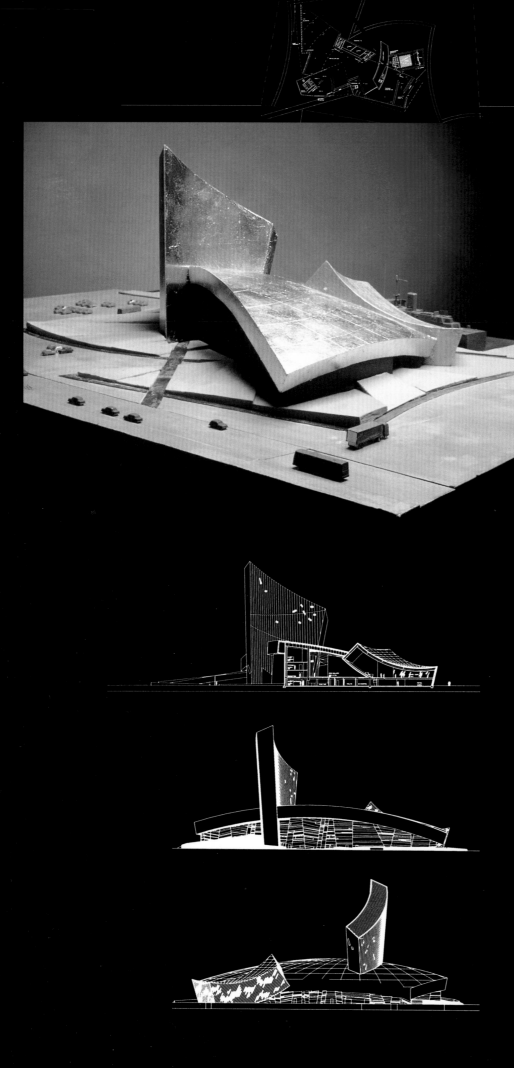

Daniel Libeskind, Imperial War Museum for the North: plan and model (top); model view (centre); section and elevations (bottom left); and earth shard sphere of plan view and canal elevation (bottom right). The war museum was one of the schemes which was rejected for funding by the Heritage Lottery Fund.

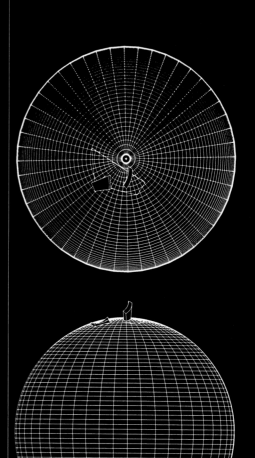

They did back it then, but proceeded to 'review' it in June of 1997, so it was not until June of that year that politics gave us the final go-ahead. For the team to come together, to stick to the Circle of Time, to design the Dome, to decontaminate the site, to prepare the work and to start building – which they had to do – when they still didn't know if they'd have a job after May of that year was phenomenal. The project at the moment is on time – at the last count it was two weeks ahead of time – and it's still on its £758 million budget. It is not over budget or delayed. Since everybody who confronted this project two or three years ago bet money – not much I may say – that it would be late and over budget, it's a major achievement on the part of the team that they have not fallen into either trap.

Is it worth it, however? The fact that the Dome is not late and is on budget has, I think, naturally led my naturally sceptical profession, and many of yours, to try and find something else to complain about. All right, you build a great dome; all right, it represents the height of architectural talent in Britain, as does the underground station and Norman Foster's shed over the top of it – three stupendous works of modern architecture on any reckoning; all right you've achieved all that. We expected that of you. What are you going to put inside it? I was interested in what Peter Murray said about the Festival of Britain (see p6). Nobody remembers what was inside the Dome of Discovery; they just remember the Dome of Discovery and the pylon. We have here a curious mixture of the Dome of Discovery and 12 pylons, but it still is essentially a dome; it is essentially the same building. It is not surprising since we had to proceed with the building when we had a date as we did. We had to make absolutely sure we were on target with the building even if we had not proceeded that far with content contracts.

But the additional problem was that it wasn't until June of 1997 that we could let content contracts, because it wasn't until June 1997 that we knew if we were going to go ahead. It wouldn't have been remotely responsible to let those contracts. But the concept under which those contracts were let was still the same as for the Circle of Time: Who are we? What do we do? Where do we live? This concept was broken down into 12 or 14 subgroups. They are still robust; they weren't changed by Peter Mandelson; they weren't changed by the incoming government, nor were they changed by any architectural variations in design. They are where we started and where we mean to end.

At this point we encounter the natural next step in the critical mode. Not enough, we were told, had been revealed about what's going on in all these zones. There should be more bottom-up design, or perhaps there should be greater top-down authority. Why, we were asked, isn't there a strong person leading all this? The fact of the matter is that we did leave this to the competitively selected designers to interpret as they chose architecturally. They should come forward with their proposals – as to how they would see the design profession interpreting these particular concepts. That is what is now happening.

There isn't a single person associated with this project who hasn't been screaming at the designers week in, week out to show us what they're doing, but as long as they're on time I will defend the rights of designers not to reveal work to the public until they've finished it. Every month more designs are finished. A month ago we showed about half of them, some of them still in outline, to the press and public. I think that was the right thing to do, because it's public money, and people are entitled to see what is being done with their money in so far as we can show them. But the design project is still on critical path, and it's on budget. If I was a designer I wouldn't want to have all of you crawling over my work before I'd got something that I was prepared to show. I think it's an insult to Eva Jiricna, Zaha Hadid and the hundreds of young designers who are working on this project to say they're no good, because you haven't seen their work yet. There has been, if anything, a bias towards the younger design teams. There's certainly been a bias towards a certain amount of risk. They have been told unashamedly that this is not a trade fair, nor is it a funfair. They've got to straddle this very difficult divide.

It would have been quite irresponsible, I think, for us to have done what Stephen has now said he wanted to do, which is to go to a sponsor and say, you have the zone. You would have got exactly what Peter was complaining about: logo-itis all over it. There has to be a relationship between a sponsor and a zone, and there is such a relationship. The sponsorship is not going badly at the moment. It's going better than most people would have expected. But there is always going to be a tension between a sponsor and a designer, and it's right that there should be. You will doubtless read many stories over the next six months of rows between sponsors and designers. All I can say is that those tensions are inherent in this sort of exercise. At the end of the day our objective at the Commission was to make quite sure that we did not have something that was an easy road – a Hanover Trade Fair – nor something that was Battersea Funfair, not even something that was just a static exhibition.

If we made any decision it was that it would not be about the past. The whole of Britain in the year 2000 is going to have exhibitions about the past. Every museum is planning one. Had we decided that we were going to do one too I think we'd have been excoriated. We were going to do the most difficult thing, something about the future. That is the remit that's been given to these designers, and its a difficult remit for them to carry out. There will, as they say, be thrills and spills, but the criteria the Commission wanted from this project above all was that it be bold, that it take some risks, that it be big and brash, but also reasonably subtle. I think that some of the designs that you've seen so far fulfil that remit; some of them possibly don't; and there's still time to work on them. If we were running crazily behindhand, or running crazily over budget, or if the Commission was worried that this show was being sold out to commercial interests or to Disneyland, then we at the commission would be calling a halt. As it is, we are content with what's being done. I personally am very excited by it, and I think on the day, when you see many things that will not be revealed until the day, you will feel the same.

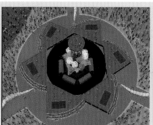

HELEN CASTLE – *CURATING THE DOME*

Once the Millennium Dome had been designed by Richard Rogers Partnership, the exhibition organisers were left with the daunting prospect of filling an area of 80,000 square metres with a contents that would be totally inclusive – which would please, entertain and educate everyone. Helen Castle spoke to the Dome's Production Director Claire Sampson and Contents Editor Martin Newman, in order to find out about the process that the New Millennium Experience Company has undertaken to develop and refine the 15 zones.

All the way along, curating the Dome has been a matter of building consensus. Consensus among a huge number of advisers, writers, designers, theatrical organisers, architects, engineers and contractors; above all, consensus among the public. For the entire spectrum of the British public has to be accommodated by the Millennium Experience at the Dome if the target of 12 million tickets sold in a single year is to be reached. (The number of rides, for instance, has had to be restricted to take into account the elderly and disabled.) More than this, however, the Dome has to square itself with the British people at large to justify itself and its enormous expense. The vocabulary of this curatorial process of consensus may be totally New Labour – 'godparents', 'litmus groups' and focus groups – but it is advocated with undeniable passion. On site, in the presence of Claire Sampson and Martin Newman, it is difficult not to believe their claim that the result of involving such a wide range of people with different perspectives, not generally involved in exhibitions, will leave an enduring legacy on the design industry. And will, in a sense, become a self-fulfilling prophecy.

In effect what Sampson and Newman are indirectly claiming to have done under the leadership of Jennie Page at the NMEC is to have taken the government prerequisite for consensus and turned it into a highly creative, collaborative process. This has had a lot to do with their approach to the project and also the way they have attempted to turn time constraints to their advantage. The option of writing detailed design briefs for the zones was never available to them. They had to demand that their designers worked collaboratively with them, simultaneously looking at ideas and experiences. The contents editors of the Dome therefore never talked about being curators in the traditional sense. They were far removed from the conventional curatorial role of selecting specific objects. (In fact Martin Newman, who works across zones and has direct responsibility for Mind, Shared Ground,

Living Island and Journey, does not have an exhibitions or museums background but was for many years a senior writer at Imagination.) The editors cast themselves as conductors or sound technicians in the process. This was, apparently, where Stephen Bayley came unstuck as the Dome's Creative Consultant. As a very successful art curator at the Boilerhouse in the V&A, he was unwilling to surrender or revise his working methods, preferring to produce in-depth briefs for designers.

In line with the NMEC's policy of concurrence, the starting point of the zones was market research. People were asked what the Millennium signified for them: 2000 years on from the birth of Christ, the triumph of Western capitalism, an excuse for an enormous Hogmanay? For many it seemed to represent the biggest New Year's resolution ever – an opportunity to completely review themselves. The single line which emerged out of focus group discussion, and was physically said in a group was 'Time to make a difference'. This helped to crystallise the organisers' approach. Sampson, who joined Jennie Page at the Millennium Commission, previous even to the founding of the NMEC, admits that Page and herself already had a clear emotional vision prior to this, but that this further focused it. For them it was always going to be a project about a nation's sense of itself. In de Toqueville's words, it was all about 'fearing to fall, hoping to rise'. They now had a strong sense that in offering people a good day out at the Dome they would be able to inject some positive thinking into people's lives. This was more than conjecture, they talked to a lot of people who had visited the Festival of Britain in 1951 and who still regarded it as one of the most special days in their lives.

The leap was made from the single line or hook, 'time to make a difference', to the zones' individual themes by breaking it down into three strands: who we are, where we live and what we do. These became building blocks for the 15 zones, which all fall into one of these three categories. It was essential that the design of each zone, particularly those with more intellectual themes such as Mind and Faith, was integral to its content. The collaboration of consultants and advisers became a necessity for each zone. The Mind Zone designed by Zaha Hadid, for instance, represents a bridge between art and science. The creative aspect of the brain is represented by artists who were selected by Doris Saatchi, who were able to demonstrate a flair for site-specific, thematic – specific pieces. Brain science and robotics are also important features. Professor Richard Gregory, a world authority on the brain and perception and the founder of the New Bristol

1 Home Planet	7 Work / Learning	13 Mast Way
2 Living Island	8 Mind	14 Money
3 Shared Ground	9 Faith	15 Our Town Story Theatre
4 Play	10 Self Portrait	16 Rest
5 Body	11 Journey	17 Talk
6 Main Entrance	12 High Way	18 The Millennium Show Arena

Science Centre, was appointed the zone's godparent. All zones, with the exception of Rest, have godparents: Chris Frayling is the godparent of Faith; Professor Sir Michael and Catherine Peckham, eminent surgeons, are godparents to the Body; and John Sorrel of the Design Council is godparent of Self Portrait. Referred to for their specialist knowledge, godparents additionally act as ambassadors for the zone at a senior level. Many of them also sit on a further consultant body, the Litmus Group, a creative review panel to which all the concepts are presented. Chaired by Michael Grade, it includes the likes of Alan Yentob, Michael Jolly and Richard Rogers.

When the Dome is opened on 1 January 2000 it may not have an single architectural masterpiece at its centre comparable to the Barcelona Pavilion, which Stephen Bayley advocated, but the rigorous working practices of its organisers will mean that they can truly claim, in Tony Blair's words, to have been 'tapping in to the creative talents of the British people'. These include token focus group members, as well as designers and dignitaries. Whether the combined impact of the Dome and all its zones will truly give children 'an experience so powerful and memories so strong' and an 'abiding sense of purpose' remains to be seen.

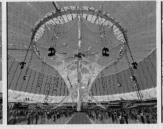

NIGEL COATES
THE BODY ZONE

The Body Zone has allowed Nigel Coates to tackle issues of gender and identity, and the representation of the human figure in art over the last thousand or so years, in a structure some 27 metres high. Here Charles Jencks interviews Nigel Coates on his portrayal of the ambiguously sexed reclining body and the design evolution of the zone.

CAJ: The Millennium Body is a much more controlled celebration in ritual, partly due to necessity – to time constraints and budget. Can you describe its evolution?

NC: The original design was a semirealistic, seated figure, with arms clasped around the left knee, and looking past a child, that was, in some way, in his care. The debates on the body were mostly centred around the question of its sex; there was a fear over whether it was male or female. Also, was it a member of the government? What did it represent? We couldn't say: 'Oh, it's the body, as in an anatomical textbook.' Rather it was a representation of both an individual and collective aspiration towards the next century and the Millennium. I focused on one of the major trajectories in our attitudes to the body this century, the question of gender, of how men and women consider each other. There's been a great deal of work done in the art world on the politics of the body, about claiming the body as yours; and that tipped over into the fashion world with tattooing and body adornment etc. These are all aspects of different attitudes towards our bodies and who we are.

CAJ: Adolf Loos argued that ornament and tattooing the body are signs of regression, and that today we don't have need of ornament and tattoo because we have higher pleasures, abstract pleasures. Anyone who tattoos their body, he said, is either a degenerate aristocrat or a criminal. In resurrecting the body and ornament you have gone against one of the foundations of Modernism.

NC: Le Corbusier looked at the body as a symbol, as a measure of all the things we have talked about, but not as a unit of feeling or pleasure.

CAJ: Which is why this country has been wound up over the sex of the Millennium figure. It's been both titillating and a hard question to answer. Your solution is a kind of double. Not only is it hermaphroditic, but it could also be read as a couple engaged in play and sex, or at least embracing. I understand you have consciously designed a reclining rather than dominating figure, an avoidance of the power figure, the Colossus.

NC: Yes, we don't want a Nazi or Stalinist figure.

CAJ: You are saying: 'We today are not the statue of Rameses, not the statue of Zeus. We are a double figure that is much more engaged in relaxation and interaction.' Clearly that's your intention. The only critique, then, is the missing detail – the nipples, the eyes.

NC: It's intended to be sensuous and sensual in another way. It's about energy and an understanding of the courage in acknowledging the differences and similarities of our bodies.

CAJ: You have avoided the problem that always comes up in public art, 'What do we do with the fig leaf?'

NC: Funnily enough, it didn't come up because as it developed the sex became more abstract. This, in a sense, acknowledged the fact that it is as much a building as it is a sign or a piece of sculpture. It is not meant to be a work of art. To adopt that abstract language allowed a transformation of literal representations.

CAJ: But surely one of the things about sexuality is the veiling, revealing and anticipation.

NC: But the Millennium figure is veiled in terms of its realism.

CAJ: But it may be so veiled that people aren't engaged with wanting to discover more. In your other body diagrams for furniture there is an abstraction *and* a particular musculature, for instance in the eyes and the senses.

NC: We've tried to balance between those two poles so the mood of the figure is soft and familiar. I hope that when people look at it, they will be able to identify with the mood of the composition. To invest the body with the potential to be read in double ways again comes back to the avoidance of a specific interpretation of particular body parts.

CAJ: But you need some specificallity in order to want to read it.

NC: Well I don't know if we've achieved that.

CAJ: It may be too early to say, but, why the colours blue and yellow?

NC: We wanted the colours to emphasise the form. The blue recedes and is underneath in the shadowy parts of it, while the

The interior and exterior of the Body Zone photographed 10 November 1999.

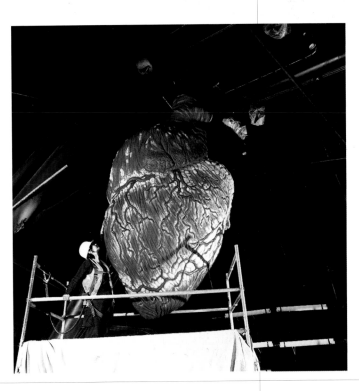

Construction in progress on the 'skeleton' of the Dome's Body Zone (left) and on the skin of the Body (below).

yellow colour advances. We don't want to be black, white or representational.

CAJ: Why the soft surface?

NC: As you approach the body you will see the shape of it and dominant parts. But as you get near, the parts will set up other avenues of intrigue, and the material will suggest tactility.

CAJ: It will cut down reverberation, which is very important. What about the neon that separates male and female, is it a kind of aura?

NC: It is an energy field, an opportunity to bring movement and light to counteract the conventional sculptural aspects of being a continuous form.

CAJ: And what does he hold?

NC: A crystal ball, a cyber-sphere, with perhaps a life-size holographic figure. That is a touchstone of scale and presence which equates with the people visiting. It brings down the scale to their scale. It's also another manifestation of light: the body as light, the body as feeling, the body as immaterial condition.

CAJ: One of the things about a Colossus is that it can be alienating and imposing, as well as inviting and empathetic. By making yours recline and embrace, it's obviously at the empathetic end of the scale. If you don't give it some kind of tactility at a smaller scale, it might be as alienating as a mannequin.

NC: We're aware of that. The actual surface must be attractive and touchable and must set off a lot of questions about what our skin is. But the importance of the actual exhibit is inside the body, and when you go inside it will explore all the different scales and manifestations of how our body works and what it feels like. We have devised spaces that are suitable for telling stories of various aspects of the body, from genetic theory to the functioning of the main organs and so on. However, as designers our main concern was to concentrate on issues of identity, feeling and empathy, using the exterior of the body. Inside the body, it's the story of contemporary thinking about the way the body works, in quite an objective sense, whereas, when one comes out of the body and into the so-called exploration zone, it will then explore specific ideas about identity, medical progress, euthanasia, body adornment, etc.

CAJ: Is there a culmination of the journey?

NC: You get a kind of interlude. When you come out of the female torso you come on to the platform from which you can see the area below, which you have already crossed, or the 'world that you have left'. From the outside you'll be able to see people crossing this, which will tell you that there is a journey ahead. Whilst on the inside, we want you to forget about the frame of the body because you are overtaken by the sort of nightclub, non-space where the story takes over.

CAJ: Will it be dimension-less, with dark curved surfaces?

NC: Yes. The movement will be continuous and very controlled; three and a half thousand people will go through every hour. This will be a Piranesian kind of space, a lost space and a gigantism mixed with massive shows about processes that go on in the body. It will have a cathedral-like quality, although not tangibly architectural like, say a Gothic structure. It will be more abstract than that, and deliberately scale-less. The experience of going inside your own body, and that comes back to ecstasy. How? On the level of the sign, of what it feels like, but also on the level of the journey through the choreography.

CAJ: You work with other artists, and you have taken a lot of your ideas literally, from other artists. Of course, in the past, architects *were* artists.

NC: It's been incredibly important to find new ways in which the architectural reality can actually communicate and enlist people's experiences that aren't necessarily architectural. To explore ways of creating a commonality between people and the environments that they're in. Artists, in their role as commentators and facilitators of how we see the world – but don't realise it – open doors and allow us to be more conscious of ourselves. The work of many artists has enabled me to get into a new mind-set, a new route of exploration that would not have been possible through the culture of pure architecture.

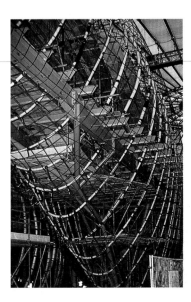

ZAHA M HADID
MIND ZONE, MILLENNIUM DOME

Presented with one of the most abstract and intellectually challenging zone subjects, Zaha M Hadid from the beginning formulated a strong design vision for the Mind. Here in a text specially prepared for Architectural Design *by Hadid's office, it is explained exactly how they approached the zone.*

Both in their winning competition entry and subsequent work on the Mind zone, the office of Zaha Hadid proposed a way of working with both the content of the exhibit and its structure as a complete idea. This approach of exhibit selection with structural design has evolved an integrated design for a complex subject matter. The design represents the dichotomy of the subject matter. How to represent the mind when its physical manifestation of the brain is an inadequate signifier of the complexities of the mind? When the mind is mostly an experiential consciousness, its physicality can only be seen as a host mechanism. The design attempts to reflect this idea. The exhibit structure of folding, continuous surfaces is seen as a host, the physical presence on which and within which the content can be located. The various exhibits are seamlessly embedded into the moulded surfaces of the structure. The overall experience is articulated as a rhythmic relief moulded from a single continuous substance rather than being segmented into distinct autonomous rooms. The folding structure offers a spatial interplay and confrontation with the subject matter which strives to stimulate the participant to think.

It was the strategy to avoid an overtly pedagogical feeding of the audience; instead, the audience was to be interactive in the oldest sense of provoking thought. It was because of this underlying premise that artists were proposed as the main exhibitors. Artists were selected whose works dealt with these issues and were invited to create specific installations for the zone. The exhibit is organised around their propositions, which lead a participant through the exhibit by conditional stages: from the question of what constitutes intelligence to perceptual inputs, through the mechanisms of thought to speculations on cultural/individual malleability. Throughout it there is the understanding of an ability to avoid the restriction and reduction of definitions that prevent any mind from evolving and progressing.

The client sought from this proposal an opposite so that the evocative is juxtaposed with the explanatory. The ambiguity of the subjective artwork is interplayed with the intentionality of the scientific device or application. Issues are raised directly by the capabilities of an infrared camera or the complexity of organisational methodologies. Nothing is hermetically sealed so neither art nor science is seen in isolation, self-contained items without other frames of reference. Their very juxtaposition in the exhibit allows neither the entitlement nor privilege of a position. This takes away boundaries or inhabitations associated with both so that they become exposed to a wider public inquisition. The audience is free to explore both as propositions and come to their own conclusions.

By the usage of evolutionary materials the exhibit integrates the content with the structure into a singularity. The materiality is focused on the synthetic, the mind made materials of the present. The brief to create a continuous floor/wall/soffit has produced a unique lightweight transparent panel made from glass-fibre skins with an aluminium honeycomb structure. Similarly the base steel structure is layered with translucent materials, which seek to create an ephemeral temporal quality.

Experience of the exhibits is intrinsically linked to how the space allows the audience to occupy it. When the participant is conscious of an overtly premeditated routing the restriction implies that the space has been quantified to suit and flow optimisation. The exhibit design resists this approach by creating as open and fluid a sequence of spaces as possible. The visual porosity of space allows anticipation of exhibits as well as looking back on to exhibits already encountered from a different perspective. The form, however, can never be anything but deterministic in its approach. It does not give a total freedom but creates the possibility of imagining such a freedom. The exhibit in the end becomes an exploration of limits where the abstract can only be reached through the tangible.

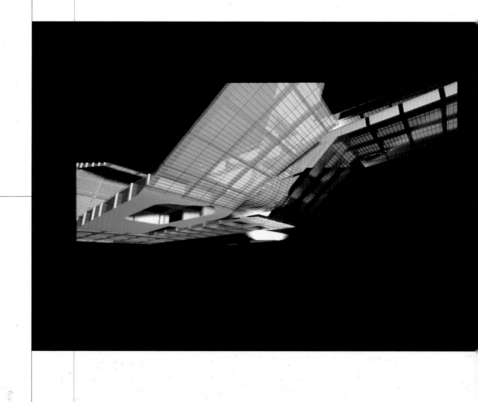

Zaha M Hadid, computer-generated
images of the Mind Zone.

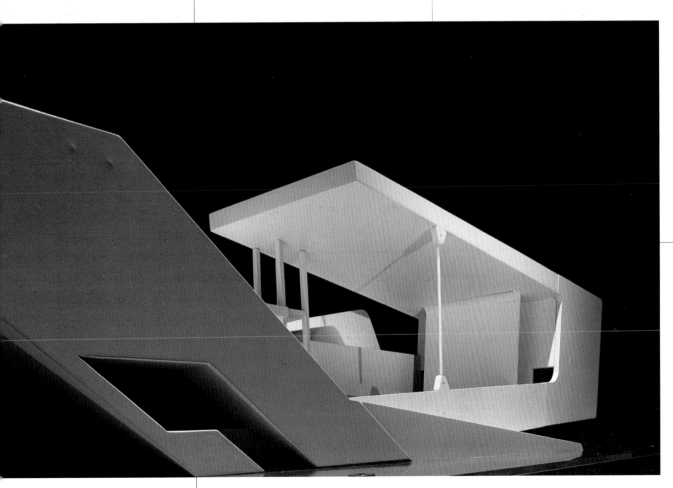

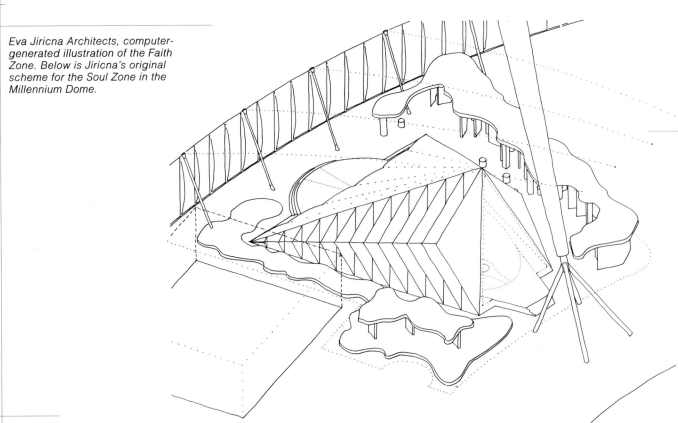

Eva Jiricna Architects, computer-generated illustration of the Faith Zone. Below is Jiricna's original scheme for the Soul Zone in the Millennium Dome.

EVA JIRICNA
FAITH ZONE

For Eva Jiricna the design evolution of the Faith Zone – previously known as the Soul or Spirit Zone – has been a Kafkaesque journey. The spiritual and potentially religious content has made it the most contentious zone, and the focus of attention for those who are concerned with the Millennium as a sacred festival. During the lead up to 2000, the Dome's organisers have been under considerable political pressure to represent the Christian dimension in their celebrations, while also including other faiths. Jiricna gave Helen Castle her own account of the story of the zone.

In September 1997, Eva Jiricna devised a total concept for the Soul Zone. It was the result of a considerable amount of thought and research: among her sources in the original written proposal for the zone, she quotes Mathieu Ricard and Paulo Coehlo, and perhaps most pertinently and evocatively Antoine de Sainte Exupéry's *The Little Prince*; the philosophy of the classic tale provides the unlikely but convincing inspiration for a scheme which requires universal appeal, transcending age and cultural background. It was also in line with the New Millennium Experience Company's vision of the Millennium: 'Who we are, where we live and what we do.' With the Mind and Body Zones it formed the first part of the tripartite maxim. In line with this Jiricna's proposal for the Soul reflected the generic and human aspect of people. It emphasised the collective, common aspects of humanity rather than the differences between people. It was intended to bring out the good in people and project an optimistic image of the future. Jiricna divided the zone up into three distinct areas: 'the search for humanity', 'celebration of all aspects of life' and 'the garden of joy'. The search for humanity echoed the NMEC's notion that the Millennium should be a time of reflection and review. When entering the zone people would be confronted with views of themselves both literal and distorted in mirrors, so that they would have to find their true selves; on leaving they would have crossed over a glass bridge. 'Celebration of all aspects of life' was to be a place for meditation and peace. Like Tadao Ando's Meditation Space at UNESCO it was to be a place for prayer, or just quiet, transcending religious, ethnic and cultural differences. 'The garden of joy' was to complement it by being a space in which to celebrate nature by bringing people into contact with plants and flowers in a tranquil environment. Like some of Itsuko Hasegawa's most successful public projects, it was to create a sensory landscape out of the real and the artificial.

The main structure of the zone was to take the geometric form of a pyramid. With its triangular planes it was chosen for its harmonious connotations; throughout history the triangle has been used to represent harmony. An outer fabric on the triangular roof was to provide soundproofing from the general bustle of the busy Dome outside. Within the pyramid itself was a convex egg or platform made of stone, surrounded by water with a channel running through it, which was to provide seating and form the main contemplative space. The interior of the pyramid would have been either black or white and the abstract figures of the triangle and the egg were chosen as universal symbols to avoid any particular religious connotations. An awareness of the soul was to be the only prerequisite in this space and to be the unifying force among people visiting the zone. Jiricna envisaged that the only palpable presence might be music, specially composed by John Taverner for the Millennium.

The NMEC initially invested and bought heavily into this concept. Five months after the proposal was accepted in September 1997, a £6000 model was made for the zone. It was presented at the Royal Festival Hall on 24 February 1998, on the

Commemorative photograph to mark 'Faith' topping out at the Dome on 28 July 1999; below and opposite: further construction shots of the zone.

day that Tony Blair made his speech in support of the Millennium Dome. Soon after, however, it became apparent that there was a serious shortfall in funds. Jiricna's original scheme would, she estimated, have cost £7 million and, at least initially, no sponsor came forward. It was not, though, just economics that required that the original project be totally revised, if not redesigned. The particular area of the Dome allocated to the zone is directly over the Blackwall Tunnel, which meant that it couldn't take any substantial loading. This immediately ruled out the building of a solid structure. There was also a shift in the way that the Spirit Zone was being perceived by the NMEC. The curating process, which required acquiring consensus from public representatives every step of the way, meant that a large group of religious leaders from all the main faiths was being consulted, all of whom wanted a stake in the zone. Rather than seeking an intellectual level, which was to demonstrate a way forward in which people were to be unified by their common humanity, the exhibition organisers felt compelled to show themselves to be inclusive by exhibiting information about nine different faiths.

The remit for the entire zone changed as the intention of creating a space for spiritual tranquillity was bypassed by the pressing need to display as much information as possible about various faiths. Jasper Jacob Associates was brought in to design the exhibition content. The change of name from Soul to Spirit to Faith was not incidental. It shows the gradual shift towards a zone which is now largely an exhibition area for educating people about the predominant faiths in Britain today. The NMEC website currently describes the experience of the zone as one which gives the opportunity to 'explore the values that underpin our society. See how they are expressed through faith and belief'. This for Jiricna is divisionary and falls short of her original vision for a scheme that sought to look forward and unite people in a national celebration. It dwells on their differences and cultural histories rather than aiming to project them into a more positive future.

The final Faith Zone is designed largely as an exhibition area. The elements that provide one of the central focuses are the nine Life Points – glass blocks – that embody each of the nine faiths represented in the Dome. The main curvaceous structure is primarily a shade that controls the level of artificial light within the zone, and thus enables people to view the exhibits satisfactorily. The problem with loading on the site meant that Jiricna even had to fight to keep the walls which are designed to be as light as possible. At the core of the structure remains a small central space for contemplation, a scaled-down version of her original concept. It is enclosed by the same fabric as the roof with layers of gauze inside. She hopes that there will be a light installation by the American artist James Thurrell inside the structure.

Ultimately Eva Jiricna wishes that the politicians had had more conviction, that they had been able to sustain their own belief in their and her own initial vision. As she has been pushed further and further away from her original concept for the zone, she has had to square her position with herself every inch of the way. She has not taken the job lightly. Designing the zone, she realises, has put her in a situation of a great deal of responsibility. She has, in her own words, sought 'step by step not to upset the souls of the future by reducing any extreme differences of opinion in architectural terms'.

August 1999

BRIAN EDWARDS

SUSTENANCE FOR THE SUSTAINABLE

Green Millennium Projects in the UK

An alternative to the sacred and outrightly secular are green schemes, which pioneer sustainable design and more often than not educate the public in environmental matters. These carry with them a sense of morality, or at least social responsibility, and a respect for the planet which is common to many world religions. Here Brian Edwards gives an overview of the development of green architecture and looks at three schemes part-backed by the Millennium Commission in Britain.

Although only 27 per cent of the projects supported by the Millennium Commission have a 'green' dimension, a number of the most prestigious ecological schemes are in receipt of some of the biggest grants. The Earth Centre in Yorkshire with a grant of £50 million and the Eden Project in Cornwall with £37 million signal the importance of environmental education buildings in shaping awareness in the next century. Whereas the Commission has given grants to 180 projects nationwide, it has reserved its biggest awards for two areas – art and ecology. Both are key elements of postmodernity and both also in their way connect us back to the more simple and harmonious state of pre-industrial times.

It is ironic that the fruits of gambling should lead to buildings whose ambitions are far from secular. The Millennium Commission has turned the Lottery card into dozens of exemplar projects which seek to re-establish contact with nature, God or the creative spirit. Communities which are divided by poverty or dereliction are being given hope by their own expression of hopelessness – gambling. Out of the wish to escape via the Lottery draw comes quite another escape – and one which embraces everybody. Through architecture and its means of expressing higher ideals, there is the prospect of social and environmental reordering. The Millennium projects are therefore more than buildings; they are the cathedrals which cradle and communicate new ecological paradigms. A project funded by the Commission which does not rise to the occasion fails in its deeper duty to society.

Like all new movements in architecture, 'green' design has a long taproot through history. Karl Marx, JS Mill, John Ruskin, William Morris and WR Lethaby all reflected upon a closer union between human development and nature.[1] Marx, for instance, predicted that growth would be limited by social and environmental constraints; Mill advocated the notion in the 1850s of a 'stationary state' economy with a fixed level of infrastructure; Ruskin said that nature provided the only lasting model for

architecture, and Morris proposed utopian artist communities in close correspondence with the land. Most telling is perhaps WR Lethaby's assertion in 1892 that by combining the aspirations of 'nature and man ... all will be sweetness, simplicity, freedom, confidence and light'.[2]

It is with a certain inevitability that the next millennium ushers in a renewed interest in ecological design. The theoretical and political momentums for change have gathered pace over the past two decades. Books such as *Silent Spring* (1962) and *Small is Beautiful* (1973) paved the way for the social change which led to the setting up of the Brundtland Commission (1987) and the UN Earth Summit at Rio (1992). Gro Harlem Brundtland, the former prime minister of Norway, is honoured with what remains the key definition of sustainable development: 'development which meets the needs of the present without compromising the ability of future generations to meet their own needs'. It should be noted that the defining statement of the post-industrial age was articulated by a woman. Gender politics, ecology and green design have together brought about a new 'cosmological symbolism' in architecture as Lethaby put it over 100 years earlier.

The Earth Summit at Rio (the UN Conference on Environment and Development) ratified the Brundtland definition and extended its influence to key areas such as climate change, biodiversity, rainforest protection and waste reduction. The agreements, signed by 180 world nations (including the UK, USA and Japan) and enthusiastically endorsed by the European Union at the Maastricht Treaty (1992), led to changes in planning policy, building regulations and government policy across the world. The fact that so many Millennium projects today have a green basis can be attributed to the influence of the Earth Summit.

Although global warming was a major preoccupation at Rio, the conference marked the important broadening of the ecological design debate. Low-energy design which had been a central concern of government bodies such as the UK Building Research Establishment, became eclipsed by the bigger and potentially more interesting picture of ecology. After 1992 architects woke up to the fact that biodiversity and global ecological health had now to be put on to the design agenda. It was a change in the thrust of sustainability which took many by surprise, especially the big practices in Europe and America.

The change from low-energy design to building forms based upon ecological principles marked also the emergence of the mature phase of green design. No longer were buildings dull and dumb low-energy boxes with the technology hidden in sandwich construction or locked away in high-performance windows, but flowering expressive structures modelled on the laws of nature.

You see the change by comparing the Foster buildings of the 1980s with those of today, and the way the current gurus of architectural form (say Alsop and Störmer in the UK and Frank Gehry in the USA) are exploiting the aesthetic potential of ecology. Fragmentation, based on nature's complexity on the one hand and the formal possibilities of the laws of biology on the other, creeping into the mainstream of practice, especially the many Millennium projects.

In the process of moving from energy-focused design to that centred on ecology, the architectural profession has realised that the green movement promises to liberate practice. Just as Ruskin noted in *The Seven Lamps of Architecture* (1849), the inspiration architects should be seeking is not found in the machine but in the 'world of flora and fauna'. The systems of ecology (or what Ruskin called the 'labour of nature'), as the recent work of Nicholas Grimshaw at the Eden Project shows, are rich in architectural potential.

You could describe ecological design as the creation of the maximum of richness and diversity using the minimum of resources, with wastes being perpetually recycled. In such a system predicated upon nature, the goal is one of ever greater beauty and complexity. In much modern architectural design there seems to be the minimum of richness and diversity using the maximum of resources with wastes rarely recycled. If you compare, say, Canary Wharf in London with 20 hectares of rainforest you gain a fair idea of the disunity between man and nature. It is a measure of how far architecture has travelled in the 12 years since Brundtland that the sealed environments of countless developments in places like London's Docklands and La Defence in Paris would be unthinkable today.

There is undoubtedly a moral current behind today's green movement in architecture. Early pioneers of green design such as Ian McHarg with his *Design with Nature* (1970) and Robert and Brenda Vale in *The Autonomous House* (1975) adopted a largely ethics-centred view. Resources were finite, land and buildings needed to coexist as a system, and nature had to inform choices. Environmental ethics began to encroach upon the largely defensive territory of professional ethics. McHarg had an influence on the landscape profession in America; the Vales and others have begun to alter our outlook in the building industry in the UK. With ethical responsibilities come potential conflicts, not least over the choice of construction materials, the repercussions of design choices in terms of CO_2 emissions, and even whether building as an activity is itself legitimate. The Earth Centre in Yorkshire seeks to come to terms with these conflicts.

The maturing of the debate (in Germany more than England)

CZWG, views of model of Green Bridge Project, Mile End Park, London.

has led to two important new dimensions for sustainable design. First, that material choice must be informed by ecological accounting. Or put another way, a building is a system of complex interactions which the use of low-energy design alone does not adequately illuminate. This has developed into useful, if sometimes frustrating dialogue about 'embodied energy', life-cycle assessment, the use of sustainability indicators and functional flexibility of the building over time.

As we learn more, the choices become clearer. First, that 'place' must inform design – place in the sense of climate, culture and local materials. Second, that embodied energy means that heavyweight materials (stone, brick) should be locally sourced but lightweight, more high-tech materials can be obtained globally. It is the dialogue between the two which is informing many recent green buildings. Third, that recycling is a choice at the beginning, not end, of the building process. To design for recycling and disassembly means respecting the capital of building materials as a resource. It leads, for instance, to a new understanding of the value of metals as recyclable materials (50 per cent of new steel in the UK is already recycled old steel). Fourth, that water matters as much as energy, and arguably more so globally. Water is the key to sustainable lifestyles – for city health, food production and personal sanitation – and water stress is a greater threat to Europe's survival than energy starvation. That is why so many recent pioneering projects (eg the Earth Centre in Doncaster and the Eden Project in Cornwall) highlight water as much as energy in the configuration of the masterplan or detailed design of buildings. Water is tomorrow's oil.

If we now know more, we certainly do not yet know enough. Sustainability is unfolding quickly, yet it is becoming tired as old clichés of building forms are repeated without development (eg the atrium-centred office block). What is needed (and what Millennium projects promise to do) is to give fresh cultural expression to the green movement. Sustainable design offers the prospect of a more beautiful, spiritually uplifting and responsive architecture. Low-energy design failed as an architectural movement because it rarely reached aesthetic heights. The buildings were earth-sheltered, largely glazed to the south (or north for an office) and predictable in plan, section and detail. Ecological design, on the other hand, offers greater formal possibilities – the richness of nature as a system provides endless new avenues to explore. The typology of green building has been liberated by the fresh breezes of the ecology movement. With this architectural liberation come new building shapes, new methods of construction, new organisation of space and function. There is in this sense a fresh order emerging – one which offers the potential to create a more humane, biologically sound and healthy architecture.

So we stand at the edge of a millennium and at the unfolding of a new movement. Environmentalism is the single most important social change in the latter half of a turbulent century. It has followed the familiar path of early pioneer, political unrest and now mainstream. The profession of architecture ignores the opportunity of ecological design at its peril. The various Millennium projects offer lessons in the practical and cultural value of sustainability. A new perception of beauty is emerging – an organic curved order which acknowledges the truth, at least metaphorically, of Einstein's curved universe, confirms Darwin's thesis that higher order biodiversity wins over lower order sameness, and gives belated form to what Frank Lloyd Wright called an 'architecture which grows like nature'.[3]

Which way we face as we tiptoe into the next millennium is not a matter of style but of environmental necessity. Sustainable design opens up new aesthetic possibilities whether linear or organic. Fresh approaches to low-energy architecture began to emerge in the early 1990s but a decade later it will be the full complexity of the ecological order which drives progressive design. As designers move from energy to ecology they realise that buildings can celebrate life itself. They become sacred not secular. So we see in current Millennium projects the dominance of symbolism over function, with buildings educating the public in the difficult interactions between man and nature. As such, green buildings are a demonstration of principle, not rational containers serving measured purposes. They are celebrations of ecological truth, reconnecting man with nature and ultimately with God. They are the cathedrals of our age: light, space and structure subscribing to fresh cosmic understandings.

Sustainable design is about demonstrating a higher goal in life and expressing it in built form. If the green Millennium projects illustrated here transcend the core principles of Modernism, they still draw upon a rational, social orientated, high technological method of building. As we enter the next century, architects carry with them the seeds of their professional redemption. The green movement has not only given Western society a new morality to curb excessive material consumption, it has gifted to architecture a new spirit, purpose and aesthetic basis.

Professor Brian Edwards is Professor of Architecture at the University of Huddersfield and a member of the RIBA's 'Sustainable Futures' Committee. He is author or Green Buildings Pay *(E&FN Spon) and* Sustainable Architecture *(Architectural Press).*

Notes

1 I am indebted here to Ian Giuliani for his paper to the World Renewable Energy Congress 1996 and his lecture 'Background to Sustainability' given at the University of Reading, 19 April, 1999.

2 William Richard Lethaby, *Architecture, Mysticism and Myth*, London, 1892, p8. See also Lethaby's, 'Architecture, Nature and Magic', *The Builder*, 1928.

3 Frank Lloyd Wright, *The Future of Architecture*, New York, 1953, p262.

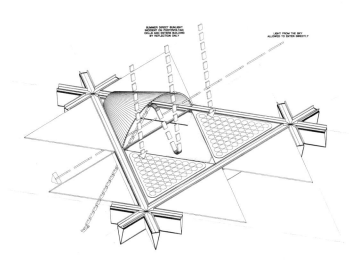

THE EARTH CENTRE, DONCASTER

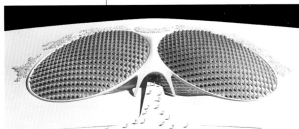

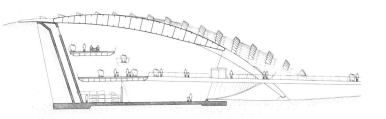

Future Systems, design for the Ark, Earth Centre, Doncaster.

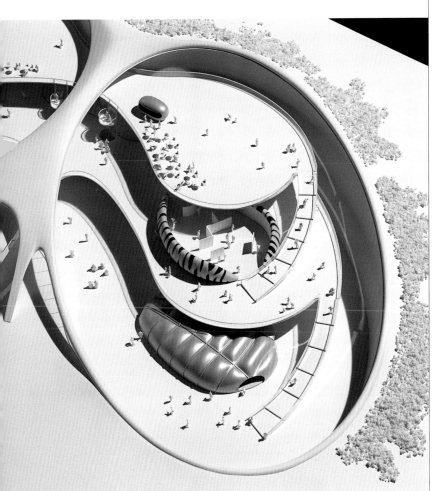

This is another Millennium project where the aesthetics of sustainable architecture are more important than the strictures of low-energy design. The Earth Centre seeks to celebrate our new compact with nature by using the medium of architecture to symbolise ecological principles. The buildings – by Feilden Clegg (who designed the influential Environment Building at the Building Research Establishment, Watford, a couple of years earlier) – Future Systems and Alsop and Störmer, with enlightened support from structural engineer Buro Happold and landscape architect Andrew Grant transcend functionalism in order to explore the more fertile territory of green symbolism. In the process the various architects and engineers involved at the Earth Centre have generated some fresh forms for the ecological design movement.

The Earth Centre has been guided to partial fruition by Jonathan Smailes, former director of Greenpeace. He took the view that there needed to be greater celebration of the green movement through architecture. His choice of designers reflects the need to market sustainability by playing the 'design' card. What has emerged to date confirms the thesis – not only are the buildings and projects spectacular as formal statements, but each in their way explores in an original fashion an aspect of sustainable design. Take for instance Future Systems' design for the Ark – a lightweight ecologically driven enclosure of 10,000m for housing multimedia exhibits on the environment. Looking like a pair of sunglasses in plan, the roof is covered in a combination of clear glass and photovoltaic panels, bathing the interior in diaphanous light. At night the building will glow like a split orange, using the electricity generated through the day via an exchange tariff with the local utility company.

Mathew Letts's building in pond (above) and Alsop
& Störmer, Waterworks (below) at the Earth Centre,
Doncaster.

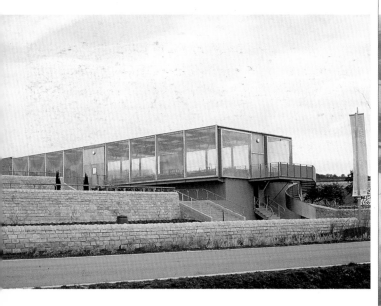

Another key building is Alsop and Störmer's Future Works tower which exploits the technology of silicon glass-fibre membranes to create a series of sun-shading skirts around the building. The exhibition space inside, on themes such as sustainable transport and future cities, is fluid, interactive functionally, and driven by environmental innovation. This is a building with an organic biomorphic profile made possible by developing new structural and cladding technologies. Ecology and High Tech make partners here.

All these buildings and many smaller structures exist as pavilions in a 160 hectare park sculpted out of a collection of former derelict industrial areas. Once occupied by coal mines, stone quarries and a glassworks, now there is nature, clear water and bio-tech buildings. The landscape masterplan evolved by Grant Associates is rich in symbolism. The majestic curves, axes and points of visual termination exist as a layer of human ambition imposed on a natural order of river flood plains, irrigation channels, water recycling reedbeds and freshly planted woodland. Man and nature are two systems which both integrate and collide, reflecting perhaps the central crisis of the 20th century. Buildings play a key role in this drama – they mediate between the worlds of ecology and industrialisation, using building design to project an image of greater harmony.
Brian Edwards

View of the site of the Earth Centre as a colliery (above), March 1993. Below is Feilden Clegg Architects, Planet Earth Galleries, restaurant and office building, Earth Centre, Doncaster.

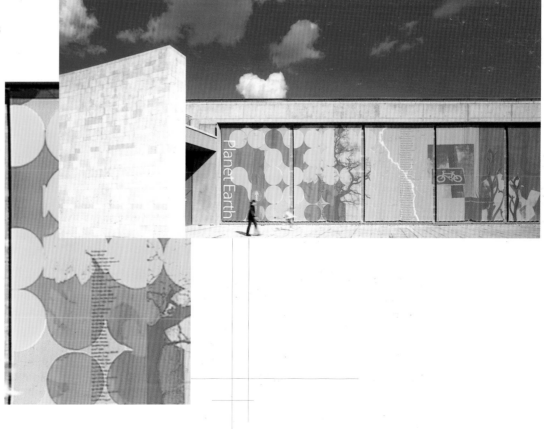

NICHOLAS GRIMSHAW AND PARTNERS

THE EDEN PROJECT
St Austell, Cornwall

Foster, Hopkins, Rogers and Grimshaw have all shown in recent buildings that high design has a role in promoting sustainability. Foster in Duisburg, Hopkins in Nottingham, Rogers in Berlin and here Grimshaw in Cornwall all play at billboarding design to show that the ecology movement is as much an aesthetic as a moral crusade.

The Eden Project in Cornwall is a huge glass vaulted series of domes set tumbling down the cliff-face of a former china clay quarry in the far southwest corner of England. On completion it will be one of the largest greenhouses on earth and a showcase of biodiversity on a huge scale. The zoophytic shape of the linked domes recalls some kind of enormous inflated intestine threaded through the landscape. Occupying over 2 hectares of enclosed space and with an internal height of 50m and the length of a kilometre, the Eden Project has a scale appropriate for the waymarking of a millennium, and a cost to match (£74 million).

As an educational building there are two messages conveyed: that of a botanical journey through habitats of distinct climatic regions (tropics, temperate zones, etc) and of an architectural journey through sustainable

Nicholas Grimshaw & Partners, site plan, visual and energy strategy for the Eden Project, St Austell, Cornwall.

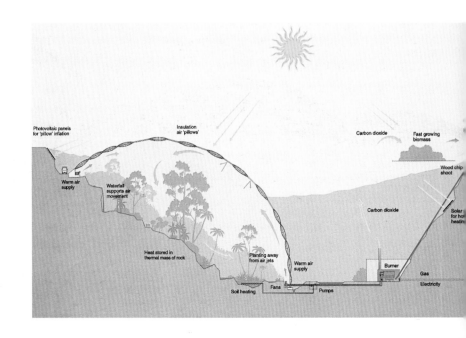

construction. The latter exploits much new technology and applies it for the first time at this scale. This is a building made of skin and structure – not form and function. The skin is flexible, responsive and changes with season and temperature. Made up of triple pillows of ETFE foil suspended beneath the steel structure on 25m x 5m modules, ETFE offers considerable advantages over glass in terms of weight, prefabrication and insulation levels. The structure itself consists of double bow-string steel trusses supported directly by the cliff-face without additional columns and foundations. Being externally exposed, the structural frame becomes a ribcage of curving members like some uncovered skeleton from *Jurassic Park*. Again, the discipline of a lightweight, low embodied energy architecture prevails.

The Eden Project faces up to the 'difficult whole' of ecological design. This is no simple low-energy building but a great, complex structure displaying in conception and detail the new organic conception of beauty. In form it draws upon biological metaphor but the discipline of construction is based upon sound building science. This is a project which not only employs suspended methods of building but seems somehow suspended between cultures. There is a sense of disbelief that crestfallen Britain can rise to such heights of architectural ambition, that what looks more like a student project than mainstream practice can actually be realised in distant Cornwall. Yet, already partially constructed, this building and its reshaped landscape promise to pip the Millennium Dome as the *Grande Project* of late 20th-century Britain.
Brian Edwards

Nicholas Grimshaw & Partners, visuals and long section for the Eden Project, St Austell, Cornwall.

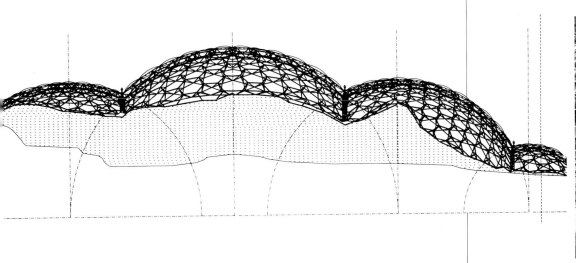

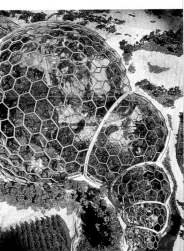

THE MILLENNIUM VILLAGE, GREENWICH

Just east of the Millennium Dome, sandwiched between Alsop and Störmer's new Greenwich station on the Jubilee Line and the muddy banks of the Thames, is the site of the Millennium Village designed by Ben Derbyshire of HTA (formerly Hunt Thompson Associates) in partnership with Ralph Erskine and the volume house builder Countryside Properties plc. The village is intended as an exemplar of sustainable development, complete with sustainable school and health centre (designed by Ted Cullinan) and sustainable Sainsbury supermarket (designed by Chetwood Associates).

The commission was won against stiff opposition from other green designers, including Foster's office. There was a significant amount of interest drummed up by the project. Andrew Wright and Associates, for instance, although they chose not to join in the competition process, developed their own design proposals, in order to forward the urban design philosophy of the practice and demonstrate how they might approach similar schemes in the future. The HTA/Erskine scheme is based upon the concept of ecological corridors which extend as fingers from the Dome. Erskine's philosophy of 'finding poetry in the economic use of resources' finds expression here in a kind of green urban lyricism. The project is intended as a model of urban regeneration exploiting the richness of the traditional European city as against the dullness of the English suburb. The Rogers masterplan for the Greenwich peninsula with its 'external rooms'

Greenwich Millennium Team, Greenwich Riverside (top), 1998, and future plan of the peninsula area (bottom) by Ralph Erskine in collaboration with Hunt Thompson Associates, 1997.

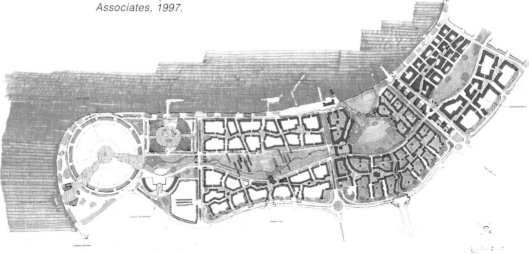

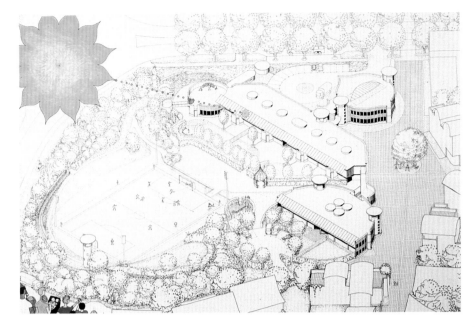

Edward Cullinan Architects, Greenwich Millennium School and Health Centre. From top clockwise: coloured axonometric, model looking east, northeast elevation, northwest elevation and southern elevation.

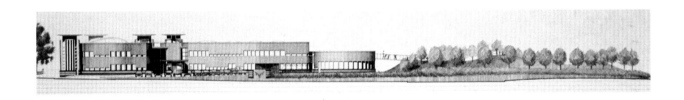

These sketches were produced by Andrew Wright Associates as an alternative scheme for Greenwich, outside the competition process.

Hunt Thompson Associates, designs for Millennium Village (top and centre) and site plan by Ralph Erskine of the Millennium Village (bottom).

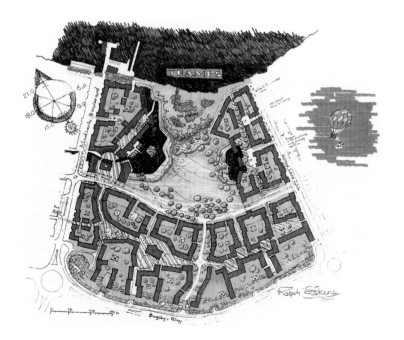

and linking 'green corridors' became the basis for the HTA/Erskine scheme. Microclimate drives the orientation and size of space between buildings (especially wind which is a major problem by the Thames), with housing blocks rising to 12 storeys as a climatic barrier on the exposed eastern edge.

The housing is stepped in form to the south to exploit solar gain and to allow overlooking of the public open space. This, like Erskine's Byker housing in Newcastle, is a blend of social and ecological idealism. Social connectivity via the medium of ecological corridors is the key, with walking and cycling the means of moving around the estate. Cars are not banned, but as at Ecolonia at Alphen in Holland and Findhorn at Elgin in Scotland, they are relegated to a minor role in the life of the community.

Lakes, parks and green corridors constitute the soft elements, stepped terraces of high-rise blocks the hard parts. Although there is an attempt to reinvent the London square as a typology of social interaction, it is the correspondence between urban housing and ecological parks which makes the project of interest to Britain as the country faces the prospect of building, according to government projections, over 4 million new homes by 2016.

Whilst the masterplan displays a latter-day revival of Ebenezer Howard's garden city ideals (as against Unwin's garden suburb which sadly proved the motor of much local authority housing pre-1950), there are modern principles at play in detailed design and construction. Following the recommendations of the Latham Committee (HMSO, 1997) the HTA/Erskine scheme exploits steel framing and prefabricated modules in order to achieve an anticipated 30 per cent reduction in building cost, 25 per cent shortening of construction time, and the minimum of on-site waste generation. This will be fast-track construction, common in housing projects in Japan, the USA and France, but rarely employed since the 1960s in the domestic sector in the UK.

Like the Eden Project and Earth Centre, the Millennium Village combines the best of high-tech construction with low-tech biological principles. Man and nature, industrialisation and ecology, establish a fresh fragile contract in these important projects. They confirm the rescuing of green architecture from the straw bale and shoddy science fringes of practice. Like Ken Yeang's work and some of Norman Foster's recent projects, they point to a century where ecological principles will generate every line an architect draws. In the process the organic will emerge, as Lethaby predicted, to give beauty to every human habitation.
Brian Edwards

Ralph Erskine, perspective of
Community Pond (top) and
sketch by Ralph Erskine for
the Millennium Village
(bottom).

Michael Hopkins and Partners, Dynamic Earth, seen from Holyrood Road with Salisbury Crags and Arthur's Seat as a backdrop.

CHARLES JENCKS

THE DYNAMIC, CATASTROPHIC, MELODRAMATIC, NOISY, BEAUTIFUL (AND KITSCH) EARTH

A visit to Michael Hopkins and Partners Dynamic Earth in Edinburgh gave Charles Jencks the opportunity to bask in cosmic pleasure, and ponder on the more pressing issues of just how good Millennium architecture can be and what sort of cosmogenic story will take the place of the Old Testament tale for further generations in ensuing centuries.

Terror, terror, *Terra, Terra.* BBC film crews chasing ITV crews chasing CNN cowboys in pick-ups racing over the flat Oklahoma plains chasing ... tornadoes – why? To get the ground zero experience, the ultimate scoop, a spinning camera going straight up surrounded by swirling dust, chickens, trees, laptops, hair curlers, cows and Wal-Mart green stamps. The Earth, Mother Earth, nasty Earth, has now emerged centre stage on TV. Competing disaster series prove it: the volcano versus the hurricane, the earthquake versus the avalanche – mud slides, floods and forest fires just don't get the ratings. But a simulation of 'the last days of Pompei', pyroclastic flow at 100 mph combined with slow, tortuous gas asphyxiation – that's living death on TV. Suddenly Mother Earth is potent again, the main actor in life's drama, as she was 5000 years ago in Neolithic culture, and there are several Millennium schemes which flirt with this idea. The first major landmark project to open, Edinburgh's Dynamic Earth, aims dead centre at this new/old genre. Is the architecture which frames the story up to the job?

Seen from the entrance side, on Holyrood Road near the Palace, the answer is a definite yes, at least for the first spectacular view.[1] Here is a dancing white explosion of sails and spikes shooting out of the ground, an eruption of ice and ashen lava, a brilliant flash against the real dark earth behind – the heroic cliffs of Arthur's Seat and its spectacular Salisbury Crags. The building, popularly known as 'Edinburgh's Dome', is much more exciting than its more famous London counterpart and, like it, is not a dome but a tent.

Michael Hopkins and Partners have designed an appropriate image and shell to celebrate the explosive earth. As well as looking like a welcoming tent, it has other overtones that lift the spirits, that strike off interesting associations. The spikes and segmental forms resemble some of the ancient creatures simulated within and, when the new Parliament is finally built directly opposite, the white sails and upturned boat hull of Hopkins's structure will complement the nautical imagery of Miralles' ship of state. Furthermore, all but one of the basic design decisions make sense. The white tent encloses the main reception area and becomes a dignified public space for civic events: not only parties and those of the annual Edinburgh Festival, but political and royal gatherings. The proximity of the new Parliament and Holyrood Palace, has already led to such bookings, and a major reason this project got Lottery funding was that its business plan was savvy about exploiting the need for civic reception space.

Mock Gothic versus tensile sails – double coding framing the crags.

Fashion shows will exploit the architectural backdrop, not to mention Arthur's Seat.

Architecturally there is one obvious precedent for Hopkins's solution. The sails of the tent fly over a massive ground plane the way the shells of the Sydney Opera House hover on a raised landform. The contrasts are also heightened here in a particularly Post-Modern way. High-Tech struts are played against heavy, ancient forms to accentuate the qualities of each. On the front, a circular entrance court, a *cour d'honneur* lacking its statue of Louis XIV, the drop-off point in contemporary bus-speak, leads to and becomes a Greek amphitheatre, only lacking its stage.[2] This theatre, with its very simple rhythmical steps, is a veritable Epidaurus in carefully sculpted stone. Its severe beauty has a gravitas that is almost heroic; it is certainly up to the other great landmarks in this proverbial Athens of the North. Around the back the masonry platform melds with the previous structure on the site, the old Scottish and Newcastle Brewery, and manages to turn its mock Gothic turrets and crenellations to something positive: a terrace framing the vista of the great crags.[3] No other city in the world has a great geological event right in its belly and, at least here, one gets a suitable celebration of it. If there is one fault of the architecture it is that the black box content of Dynamic Earth does not also exploit this presence – but more of that later.

Dissonant angles, violent contrasts, Classicism and anti-Classicism in juxtaposition (above). Dynamic Earth Brochure (below) – from the Big Bang to Homo Habilis, devolution all the way.

Michael Hopkins has, over the last 15 years, made a virtue of working both with and against the sites he has been given. It is this double-coding, done with understatement and fine detailing, that makes him the 'Mies van der Rohe of Post-Modernism'. His Glyndebourne Opera House additions, his extension at Lord's Cricket Ground, his transformation of Bracknell House next to St Paul's all fit into the past fabric, yet make subtle oppositions to it. Here in Edinburgh his double-coding is more extreme, the contrasts more tense. Fully glazed walls and fins smash right into the ground; cables, masts and white fabric curves are juxtaposed with the masonry crenellations. While the Edinburgh Classicism of circle, axis, symmetry and monumentality is carried forward, these ancient moves are countered with contemporary ones: a slash of light follows giant ribs down to an anti-Classical support. Most dissonant are the masts and entrance spikes which are rammed into the oh-so-tasteful surface, Punk jewellery meant to draw blood, to be painful.[4]

Hopkins sees contrast as the defining quality of the city: 'Edinburgh's much-admired urban character comes from a balance between nature and artifice ... ' His artifice strikes just the right note of gravitas and celebration, civic propriety and cosmic pleasure.

Post-Millennial Depression

Yet lurking behind this judgement is a definite 'but', the suspicion that, at half the cost of Frank Gehry's Bilbao, this Dynamic Earth is not quite half as good. It is not so much the building as the commission itself, and that makes you think about the architecture of the Millennium as a genre, the best of Britain's best – Foster, Rogers, Hopkins, Grimshaw, Farrell and others – which is not so bad. But neither is it very good, certainly not as good as a 2000-year liftoff demands, the cultural opening to the next thousand years, the transition from Christianity to something else. The reason for this is not so much to do with the architecture as with the process by which the projects were chosen and constructed. By necessity, by funding and countdown to an impossible deadline, there was only one outcome possible, when, in the late 1990s, most of the 28 landmark projects got under way: Risk-Free Architecture (RFA). This genre of building occurs when the following conditions are present: 1) an impossible deadline; 2) several corporate clients demanding predictability; 3) big government and big spending – landmarks are £30+ million; 4) confused content and lack of belief in anything but 'theming'; and, most of all, 5) the motive that has driven the Disney Corporation for the last 20 years 'entertainment architecture'. Yes, RFA is just entertainment architecture, its slick commercial vulgarity subtracted. Most of the time. To Hopkins's credit he has steered his way around most of these obstacles, except the one over which he had no influence: the black box operators, Disney's Imagineers, those virtual simulators that threaten the typical £50 million landmark with a case of Post-Millennial Tension.

Infotainment

The brochure and pocket guide to Dynamic Earth says it all. Jumping out of an acrid yellow background and, literally, off the top of its front page, is a lasciviously grinning teenage idiot with bulging eyes, flaring nostrils, a suitably shrunken cranium and the kind of leathery brown skin you get from too many days on the Cote d'Azur without factor 16.[5] No, this is not what adolescents become if they watch too much TV, it's not one more disgusting

Olympic mascot, it is our friend (and ancestor) *Homo habilis* – poor old adolescent fellow. When you pull the accordion-brochure to its full length, you understand where he comes from and 'how we got here and how the earth will evolve in the future' (in the memorable, opening sobriquets of the Rt Hon Chris Smith MP, Chairman of the Millennium Commission). No, I didn't make that up, I heard it and it's written in the press release: 'As we approach the millennium it is important that we understand the origin of the Earth and how it will evolve in the future.' Yeah Man. Had he visited the Dynamic Earth before he wrote those fateful lines, perhaps he would have understood something more about dynamic chaos and unpredictability – but then, on such occasions, understanding is asking too much.

The view of evolution put forward by the Edinburgh Imagineers runs in a straight line from what they call, mistakenly, the BIG BANG to a real grinning adolescent. This is the old story of progressive evolution barrelling along its path from the first prokaryote cell to a furrow-browed trilobite to a cross-eyed Icthyostega and the ever-dripping jaws of T-Rex. The actual 90-minute journey through cosmic history is better than this, and sometimes informative. Ocean depths are simulated through film seen through portholes of a yellow submarine, a tropical rainforest is simulated with fibreglass trees and interactive consoles. There is the usual earthquake simulation of earth centres (floor jiggles, smoke emerges, floor groans) and some pleasantly original surprises such as a 'real ice' iceberg (by then one is so anaesthetised by simulation that to run one's hand over the kind of smooth frost that builds up in your freezer is as exciting as your first kiss). The most convincing entertainment is a low-level fly-past between mountain peaks, a wrap-around panoramic experience of being in the nose of a helicopter as it skims close to the kind of crags you can find just outside the black box.

If, in these few cases, virtual reality is more scary than real reality, in most it is more anodyne. Ugly, flat, clichéd, even worse than a film on the Discovery Channel. The press release boasts 'cutting edge scientific thinking and up-to-the minute information from the most respected sources around the world, including National Geographic, the BBC, Reuters and NASA'. What? Scientific thinking – from those sources! 'Up-to-date'? They might have checked their story line, around which everything revolves, of a 15-billion-year-old universe. By May of this year the consensus of science – and four different methods for measuring age – put the universe's birth at between 12 and 13.5 billion years ago. Too bad, off by 1.5 billion years – at Edinburgh University that's a flunk. This lapse, however minor, points to a more general problem: the triumph of entertainment, over both science and, more importantly for a cultural institution, a poetic interpretation of the universe story.

As the reader will find elsewhere in this issue, I am in agreement with the basic idea of Dynamic Earth: the narrative of the cosmos – cosmogenesis – is our version of the Genesis story and it deserves the attention, and money, being thrown at it in the landmark projects. I, like the rest of the world, want to know how to think and feel about the important things – evolution, deep time, the significance of life and death. But the imagination and understanding of the Imagineers are not equal to the Old Testament scribes or their King James counterparts. What we get in place of biblical poetry and vision are squalid metaphors and pre-teen thrills. The universe, scientists please note, did not start in a BIG BANG (their capital letters). It was not BIG, it was smaller than a quark. It was not a BANG (no one heard it, noise

was not possible at this point and, more importantly, it was the stretching of space very quickly, faster than the speed of light). I am just giving the standard model of inflation, the consensus. All right, the birth of the universe was hot, but it didn't go off the way it appears in the Dynamic Earth simulator (as an oversize firecracker).

Scientists, like the BBC, National Geographic et al, should look at the way their metaphors have been shaped by the Pentagon and adolescent culture. It is not a pretty sight, and it alienates people from the very universe story they want to tell.

Misfired metaphor is a consequence of Infotainment, but another drawback is the way one is pushed, by a 90-minute journey, through 15 billion years, from one clichéd experience to the next, never having time for reflection. Here the black box

The poetics and patterns of rock versus culture are brought together by exhibits and structure.

approach, the programmed sequence of simulation, might have been suitably broken for those who want to meditate on such events as mass extinction, five of which have been recently well recorded by scientists. A break, at this point, from cometary collisions and volcanoes might have been apt and refreshing; a little glance at the old evidence outside, those awesome Salisbury Crags, where earth, geology and extinction are palpable. One might have broken the simulation-journey at four or five points with real touchable rocks – as the earth galleries do in London – or have actual fossils rather than fibreglass ones (real trilobites have been on sale just down Holyrood Road at Mr Woods' Fossil Shop for 25 years).

Are such sentiments elitist? Well, people have been collecting real Dynamic Earth relics for a 100 years. It is a respected custom of mass culture. What is sad about Infotainment, and so much of the Millennium Experience, is not the idea of celebrating our place in cosmic history but the way Disney methods and Science Museum techniques have dominated over other modes of conveying the message. They may have their point, and their own kind of quality, but they need the talents of a creative director who has mastered the medium. The 28 landmark projects, the universe story, have yet to produce a Truffaut or a Bergman, let alone Steven Spielberg and most of us, Post-Christians, are very much the losers.

An Opportunity Missed

The potential for this Commission, on this site, for this subject, for this date – 2000 – with £34 million to spend, was rare, indeed unique. Think of the confluence of events, some of them pure chance. A location on the most spectacular piece of urban geology anywhere; the programme to tell the universe story for the Millennium in a city noted for its great culture of science (and recently completed was the masterful six-part TV series, *Earth Story*, presented by Aubrey Manning, professor in Edinburgh); funding by the Lottery and four big corporations who had the foresight to see the potential; and, most extraordinary, as Michael Hopkins mentions in his press release: the building is 'located on the exact spot where James Hutton, the father of modern geology, lived and worked in the 18th century'.

Why is this accident of location so important? Because James Hutton, more than anyone else, was responsible for the discovery and interpretation of an unbelievable truth – at least one that could not be countenanced by Christians and those who thought the world was 6000 years old. The Bible had taught that supposition and, as Stephen Jay Gould has shown, virtually all geologists before Hutton explained a younger earth in tune with scriptural explanation of the Creation, flood and cycles of nature. The West, indeed the world in general, was not prepared for the psychological shift implied by Hutton's discovery. One can understand and relate to a universe created in six days, and considered in terms of biblical generations, even units of civilisation but, when it jumps from 6000 to millions of years, something traumatic happens to culture. We suddenly become insignificant, the universe emerges out of scale, almost out of conception. This is the revolution Hutton helped create in world thought, between 1788 and 1795, and on this site.

Think of the chance missed: it's as if the Vatican had the opportunity to build St Peter's in Jerusalem on the exact spot where Christ was crucified – did it, and then never mentioned his name! I exaggerate; there is a token mention of Hutton tucked away in back, but it took me a second visit to find it. There were others who took part in this revolution, in the forging of modern geology and our view of deep time. But this truth presents yet another opportunity missed – they also came from Edinburgh. The man who played John the Baptist to Hutton's Christ was John Playfair, much the better, and more concise, writer. Hutton's *Theory of the Earth*, a dense, 1000-page tome, was published in 1795 and rarely read, but his friend, Playfair, popularised the basic ideas in 1802 with his *Illustrations of the Huttonian Theory of the Earth*. Here we find wonderful engravings of deep time, the work of geology and its strata.[6] These illustrate the theory that the 'earth machine' or 'earth system' (today reconceived as James Lovelock's Gaia) constantly repairs itself in endless cycles. What sparked Hutton's theory were the kind of rock formations one can see around Edinburgh, and almost the kind of crags one could see out the window – if only one could see out of the damnable black box. Horizontal layers of rock sitting on vertical, up-thrust layers of rock. Hutton's theory? That the earth machine has endless three-part cycles: the erosion of rocks, their deposition in horizontal strata, and then their uplift. That is why one sees, in the famous engraving of *Hutton's unconformity*, at the top of a cliff, a horse approaching a carriage, trees, bushes and living earth: the present; underneath this are sedimentary layers of another geological era; and underneath this are some vertical striations of yet another period.

One period lays down strata through erosion, they settle on the ocean floor, then, because of pressure Hutton thought, heat up, expand and push up the mantle above: hence the unconformities of structure. The implication was that these rock cycles went on forever, and therefore that the earth was infinitely old and self-repairing. When Hutton saw the Scottish crags at Siccar Point, 20 miles from Edinburgh, through the lens of this theory they had an immediate impact, the British equivalent of Nietzsche's 'death of God'. Playfair describes the implication in an often quoted literary passage:

> On us who saw these phenomena for the first time, the impression will not easily be forgotten ... We often said to ourselves, What clearer evidence could we have had of the different formation of these rocks, and of the long interval which separated their formation, had we actually seen them emerging from the bosom of the deep ... Revolutions still more remote appeared in the distance of this extraordinary perspective. The mind seemed to grow giddy by looking so far into the abyss of time.

If Existentialists ever since have looked at rocky outcrops and seen this melancholic abyss our age, with a different theory of the earth machine – Gaia – sees a more exciting vision when it looks at crags, and this prompts a view of what the Dynamic Earth might have looked like. Instead of being alienated by catastrophes, one can empathise with processes going on, all the time, underfoot; instead of turning tornadoes and mud slides into spectacle-TV, one can take an aesthetic delight in the emergent patterns; instead of disinterested observation, one can find a poetic expression for each of nature's qualities.[7] In his Poeme Electronique for the 1958 World's Fair in Brussels, Le Corbusier designed not only an exciting, soaring, hyperbolic paraboloid of a building but, along with others, a light and sound show that made aesthetic and spiritual sense of the cosmos. Where is our Le Corbusier today, where is the artist, architect or entrepreneur with a cosmic vision?

The Millennium is an extraordinary commercial and PR opportunity. It's a marketing pitch that brands will just not be able to resist. The Design Council of Great Britain has devised a scheme called Millennium Products to promote over 600 British-designed products. Hot Springs by Bisque Ltd (left) are chosen as one of the Millennium Products being endorsed by the Design Council. Above is the Millennium Products Exhibition at the Singapore International Design Forum, 21–24 October 1998.

HELEN CASTLE

MEETING THE MILLENNIUM: YEAR 2000

Celebrations worldwide

Here Millennium architecture is placed in the wider context of the year 2000's celebrations by a brief survey of some of the main international events and an account of the momentum behind them.

Even in its advent, there can be little doubt that the year 2000 will be celebrated internationally. The mass of promotional material that is being churned out as hard copy and on the Internet by government organisations and promotional bodies is already telling us that the celebrations are to be on an unprecedented scale. The Millennium Institute, which is dedicated to the promotion of 'long-term integrated global thinking', lists 10 mega-events that are planned to involve more than a million people.[1] They include: the international Earth Day 2000, Expo 2000 at Hanover, Holy Land 2000 in Israel and Palestine, Holy Year 2000 in Rome, March of the Millennium (an international 'March for Jesus'), Millennium Celebrations 2000, Olympics 2000 in Sydney, Party 2000 in southern California, Prelude to the Millennium (a gathering of Earth Spiritualists in southern California) and Times Square 2000 in New York.

Although in 1999 these events exist in real time as no more than fixtures advocated by a mass of promotional literature, the weight of the West's investment in the Millennium means that it cannot fail to be anything but totally pervasive and all-encompassing. For the media and commerce it presents unrivalled publishing, production and business opportunities. For the usual mass of reviews, retrospectives and future predictions, which are regurgitated at a single year-end by newspapers and broadcasters, can only be paltry when compared with that of a thousand years. The bimillennium is a marketing pitch that commerce just won't be able to leave alone – even at the risk of inducing Millennium fatigue. Almost every type of product will be endorsed by some kind of association with the year 2000.

However all-consuming the Millennium is in the Western world, there can be little doubt that it will have its parameters geographically. Despite the promotional idealism of organisations such as the Millennium Institute, the celebration of the year 2000 is in its genesis very much a Western event. To what extent nations beyond the Americas, Europe and Australasia will be sucked into the celebrations can only be speculated upon; it may depend largely on the force of international branding and satellite broadcasting. (An audience of 250 million worldwide, for instance, has been predicted for the coverage of Times Square in New York on New Year's Eve.) Any amount of television time cannot, however, change the fact that the bimillennium remains fundamentally Roman and Christian in origin. It marks 2000 years on the Gregorian calendar, the revised Julian calendar introduced in 1582 by Pope Gregory XIII, and 2000 years since Christ's birth. Though the calendar has been used internationally since the 18th century, the Millennium celebrations cannot have

the same resonance for nationalities and faiths, such as the Chinese and Muslims, who do not traditionally celebrate the new year on the first of January. In fact, when looked at in this light, the desire in the West to make the year 2000 a worldwide celebration emerges as a form of insidious cultural imperialism.

Imperialism, however, implies an offensive strategy or at least consciously aggressive behaviour. This is certainly not the case with the Millennium. The rush to be organised by the end of the 20th century has meant that the programme of large-scale events has grown randomly and developed in a non-ununified way, largely propelled forward by nothing more than the necessity to be ready on 1 January 2000. Common ideological strands, though, can be identified in the thinking behind most 'mega' events in the West. This is most evident in the States which has the largest number of public projects. These all display at least one of three distinct perceptions of the Millennium: first, as a spiritual celebration; second, as a commercial occasion best celebrated by a party or some other form of entertainment; and third, as an opportunity to exercise a set of worthy liberal values. Two of the most pre-publicised spiritual occasions are the bimillennial march to mark Jesus Day 2000, whose organisers claim to be able to activate 30 million people in 2000 places throughout the US in religious processions, and the Prelude to the Millennium, a proposed gathering of Earth Spiritualists (pagan, Wiccan, Shaman, Celtic, Tibetan) over the new year period at a yet unspecified location in southern California. Entertainment will also be found in all the expected places on New Year's Eve. Traditional venues such as Times Square, New York and the City Hall Plaza in Boston are preparing to celebrate on a greater scale than ever before with increased television coverage. But entrepeneurs such as Steve Leber, a former manager of Def Leopard, are also seizing the day and are organising their own extravaganzas. Leber is hosting the 'Party of the Century' at the Javits Convention Center, New York, for 30,000 at $1000 a ticket. Star acts include Sting, Aretha Franklin and Andrea Bocelli. The even more ambitious Party 2000, in southern California, is planned as a three-day festival for 2.5 million people. The US government's own response to the arrangement of such a diverse array of events has been to determine to do something 'meaningful' itself. In August 1997, President and Mrs Clinton founded the White House Millennium Council to support a wide variety of projects nationwide. The most highprofile of these include: Millennium Evenings at the White House, a cultural lecture series; Save America's Treasures, a government and private partnership to protect the US's cultural heritage; Millennium Trails, a project that will enhance trails of local and national significance; and the Mars Project, an initiative that asks students and communities to imagine a village on Mars. The programme lacks any central focus or venue – the White House aside – but is couched in noble words and has high aims. Ellen McCulloch-Lovell, the Deputy Assistant to the President and

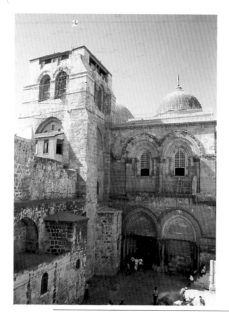

President Clinton (top) has closely aligned himself with US Millennium projects through the White House Millennium Council, which was founded by himself and the First Lady in August 1997.
Israel will be a natural magnet for Millennium fervour: Holy sites such as the Church of the Holy Sepulchre (centre), in Jerusalem, are expected to receive a record number of visitors during 2000. Holy Year 2000 will be officially inaugurated at Midnight Mass at St Peter's in Rome on 24 December 1999. More than 250,000 pilgrims came to attend the Pentecost waking (bottom), in the so-called dress rehearsal of the 2000 Jubilee with Pope John Paul II taking part in the ceremony.

Advisor to the First Lady on the Millennium, describes the Millennium Council's purpose as follows:

The theme of the White House millennium activities is 'Honour the Past – Imagine the Future.' The President has invited all citizens 'to give a gift to the future' that will strengthen our democracy, encourage citizen involvement and unleash the full creative potential of the American people as we chart our common future.[2]

Inevitably soaring eulogies part ways with what they are discussing. In this case the point of the project – a partial government scheme, contrived out of partnerships with private charities and institutions – is lost in a haze of highfalutin language.

In the main, American Millennium initiatives have tended to be independent, rather than government sponsored. They are perhaps best exemplified by the activities of the Millennium Society. The society, which was founded in 1979 by a group of Yale college seniors and claims to be the oldest organisation set up to commemorate the bimillennium, unites liberal, if rather elitist, notions of charity with the desire to host 'The Party of the Century'. The society is organising a black-tie charity benefit at Egypt's pyramids. The tickets, which are sold as travel packages ranging from $1999 to $3000, are raising money for the Millennium Scholars Program which provides scholarships to students worldwide. On booking the five-day ball trip society members are offered the additional option of attending a Millennium symposium, which brings together 'the leading minds of our time' in a peripatetic tour that travels from the foot of the pyramids, to Cairo, to the shores of the Mediterranean and Alexandria.

Though the United States has enthusiastically embraced the year 2000's political, commercial and cultural potential, it will not be the main centre of Millennium activity worldwide. Rome and the Holy Land will attract the greatest number of tourists; an estimated 15 million visitors are expected in Rome and 4 million in Palestine and Israel.[3] For the Roman Catholic Church, the Millennium is of great significance, not only as the 2000th anniversary of the birth of Christ, but also as a Jubilee or Holy Year, which is celebrated every 25 years. The origin of the Christian Jubilee lies in biblical times when the fiftieth year was proclaimed a special year by the Law of Moses. For the Church today, 'the Jublilee is a year of special grace, of remission of sins and the punishment due to them, a year of reconciliation between disputing parties.' [4] The Roman Catholic Church's calendar for Holy Years traditionally focuses on Rome as the home of the Pope and a centre of pilgrimage. In line with this the Holy Year 2000 will be officially inaugurated at Midnight Mass at St Peter's on 24 December 1999 and will be closed at the same holy basilica in Rome on 6 January 2001, Epiphany.

With the Millennium, the Church is, however, looking to place a fresh emphasis on the simultaneous celebration of the Jubilee in Rome, the Holy Land and local churches. At the beginning of July 1999, the Pope announced his intention to mark the year 2000 with a pilgrimage to the Holy Land in the footsteps of Abraham. This is intended as an outreach to the Eastern Christian Churches as well as a means of creating a direct dialogue with Muslims and Jews (Abraham is the father figure of the three monotheistic religions).[5] Controversially, the pilgrimage is starting in the city of Abraham's birth, Ur of the Chaldees in southern Iraq from where the Pope will proceed to Syria, Greece, Egypt, Israel and Palestine. Though still cloaked in secrecy, it is most probable that the Pope's visit will take place in October or November. John Paul II is already intending to visit Jerusalem, Nazareth and

Bethlehem in late March to coincide with final status negotiations between Israel and Palestine.

In Israel the momentum for Millennium celebrations has been set by the projected influx of visitors. It has been estimated that at least twice the usual number of people will visit during the year 2000. To meet this expectation hotels and extra accommodation are feverishly being built. At a conference in Spring 1999, Moshe Katsav, Israel's Deputy Prime Minister and Minister of Tourism, stated that 'Israel has invested $500 million during the last few years in preparation for 2000. It is our duty and obligation to the Christian world, and to the significant anniversary it will observe in 2000.'[6] The city of Nazareth, for instance, is prepared to reap the full potential of its biblical associations at the turn of the century with its launch of Nazareth 2000. With the aid of government grants, the city is hoping to restore its historical buildings and develop its transport infrastructure and tourist amenities.[7] The influx of foreign visitors, however, also has its dark side for the Holy Land. During the year 2000, Israel is tipped to become the prime destination for Christian cults who are observing biblical apocalyptical prophecies. This gives the Israeli security services the onerous task of policing extremist religious groups; in January 1999, the Israeli authorities were already reported to have expelled a number of cult members.[8] In Megiddo, the Israelis are planning to distract attention away from Armageddon's more gloomy associations with a party that includes light shows, holograms and period actors, and takes tourists through 6000 years of the region's history.[9]

Time is a recurring theme in Millennium celebrations throughout the world. The French, in particular, seem to have a penchant for clocks. In 1987, they first erected the Génitron to count down to the Millennium outside the Pompidou Centre (removed during renovation work in 1996). There are also plans for the Place de Concorde in Paris to be made into an enormous sundial and the Place Charles de Gaulle Etoile into a giant clock. Time is perhaps the safest card for organisers to play, allowing authorities to sidestep the issue of whether the 2000 anniversary is a sacred or secular event. The Millennium Dome has justified its location and its existence by playing on its association with Greenwich Mean Time and the Royal Observatory, and branding Greenwich 'The Home of Time'. Time, however, is limited as a *raison d'être*. It lacks Disney-like appeal and entertainment value; interestingly enough, there was never any serious discussion of pursuing time as a theme within the Dome.

The European Union has thrown its net wide for the Millennium. In November 1995, it appointed not one but nine official European Cities of Culture of the Year 2000. These include: Avignon, Bergen, Bologna, Brussels, Helsinki, Cracow, Prague, Reykjavik and Santiago de Compostela. A programme of local and mutual promotion, it is a sort of souped up twin-towns project with all nine participants cooperating in each others' projects. Santiago de Compostela is, for instance, organising a whole programme for exhibition both in its native city and on tour, with its fellow cities.

In contrast with other nations, Switzerland has opted out of the year 2000 celebrations. It is observing the start of the Millennium correctly by staging its main event in 2001 rather than 2000 (still technically the 20th century). Expo.01, not to be confused with Hanover's international Expo 2000, is 'a national exhibition with international aspirations'. Like the US's White House Millennium Council, Expo.01 refers to its Millennium initiative as a national endeavour. Through the exhibition, it claims to be examining its national identity and redefining itself and its future.[10] Expo.01 has

The Place de Concorde (top and left), in Paris, is to be transformed into a giant sundial to mark the Millennium. Santiago de Compostela (bottom) is one of nine official European Cities of Culture of the Year 2000 to be appointed by the European Union.

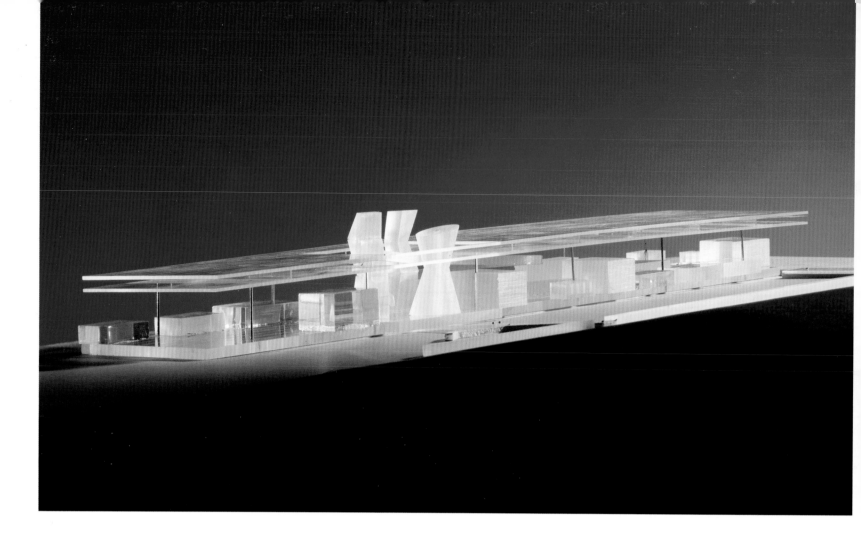

Coop Himmelblau has designed the
'Power and Freedom' arteplage
(above) at Biel-Bienne and Jean
Nouvel the mobile 'Meaning and
Movement' arteplage (opposite) for
Expo.01 in Switzerland; the Expo that
celebrates the start of the Millennium
correctly, in 2001.

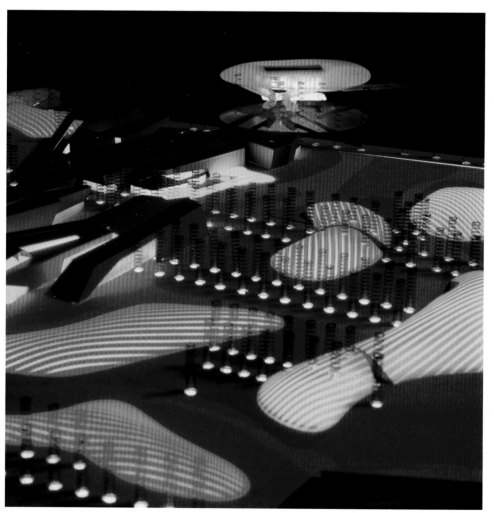

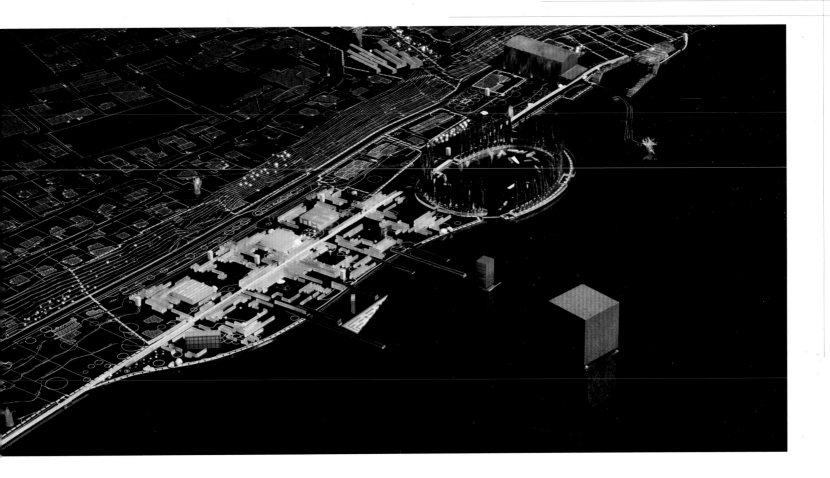

imaginatively departed from the usual convention of a single exhibition ground. It is arranged around four static 'arteplages', waterfront sites with a terrafirma 'Europark' and floating 'forum'. These are situated in the four cities of Biel-Bienne, Murten-Morat, Neuchâtel and Yverdon-les-Bains. A fifth Jura canton arteplage shuttles between the four fixed arteplages. Coop Himmelblau has designed the 'Power and Freedom' arteplage at Biel-Bienne and Jean Nouvel the mobile 'Meaning and Movement' arteplage. The remaining designs have been produced by design consortiums. Less than two years away from the event, however, it seems difficult to foresee how the contents of the arteplages will be able to live up to their idealised titles. With only 18 per cent of the expo being publicly funded, the exhibition is relying on private sources and ticket sales to fund the remaining 82 per cent. Inevitably, it will have to, at least to some extent, concede to the wishes of its 'venture partners'.

As Charles Jencks points out in his concluding essay here, 'Except for the Vatican, a quasi-nation, no country has given deep thought to what the Millennium means'. It seems, interna-tionally, that the Millennium may well manifest itself in events that are thick on rhetoric and short on content; the decision to have an event has often preceded the *raison d'être*, which is cobbled together in the rush to organise, and pumped out at full speed on all available media. It therefore comes as no surprise that the two international events which will probably be of the greatest magnitude in 2000, are held regularly, independent of the Millennium. Sydney 2000 Olympics and Expo 2000 Hanover are organised by international committees at appointed times. They may draw on the Millennium for their forward-looking imagery, and be on a greater scale than ever before, but they both have established ethoses and conventions. In comparison to the number of events already fixed and organised, very little archi-tecture is being constructed. This is because, however success-ful or unsuccessful architecture is, it requires the question of content to be dealt with. It may also just be that the honest admission that for many the Millennium can be no more than an inflated New Year's celebration may allow little scope for design-ing permanent structures.

Notes

1 For 'Millennium Alliance: Mega Events Planned for 2000', see www.igc.apc.org/ millennium/events/mega.html (last update 28 April 1998).

2 Ellen McCulloch-Lovell quoted from her letter on www.whitehouse.gov/Initia-tives/Millennium/what.html

3 See www.igc.apc.org/millennium/events/mega.html (last update 28 April 1998). Estimates of the number of visitors to both Rome and Israel vary greatly. Apparently Vatican sources have put the number of pilgrims visiting Israel during 2000 at more like 6 million, see www.journal-topics.com/travel/Israel.html

4 Extract form 'Tertio Millennio Adveniente', Apostolic Letter, promulgated by Pope John Paul II on 10 November 1994. See www.vatican.va/jubilee_2000/docu-ments/en_ju_documents_17-Feb-1997_history_en.html

5 *Guardian*, 3 July 1999, p19.

6 www.journal-topics.com/travel/israel.html

7 www.inisrael.com/tour/nazareth/project/htm

8 See *Time*, 18 January 1999, p47, and *San Francisco Chronicle*, 6 January 1999, p1.

9 www.igc.apc.org/millennium/events/israel/html

10 www.expo-01.ch/document/137.asp?

CLARE MELHUISH

ICONIC ARCHITECTURE AT THE END OF THE MILLENNIUM

International Projects for the Millennium

Can we expect the same flowering of art and architecture as experienced at the turn of the previous millennium? Could the 'festivalisation' of the year 2000 bring about a renewed emphasis on architecture as first prompted by globalisation? Clare Melhuish looks at iconic architecture at the end of the 20th century with particular reference to the Sydney Olympics, Expo 2000 Hanover and La Tour de la Terre.

The most notable aspect of the scanty public debate about the coming of the Millennium has been the lack of specificity about the purpose of the celebration, while the assumption that a celebration is in order has never been questioned. Countries such as Britain which recently witnessed a momentous change of government after many years of conservative rule, seem to have been overwhelmed by an officially sanctioned millenarianism, declaring the advent of a new age – 'the millennium', as it is called, or the 21st century – while avoiding any discussion of concrete social change, and without any reference to the past. Indeed, this is a type of millenarianism which exhibits an unusually complacent and even narcissistic absorption with the society of the present, its achievements gauged in terms of material success, and a great unwillingness to acknowledge its problems and initiate a discussion about how they might be addressed and remedied in the future.

Certain lines of anthropological research have suggested that the closely connected histories of Christianity and politics in Europe may be read as expressing a succession of millenarian waves and reactions to them – mainly generated by resistance movements of various sorts. Now we face the curious prospect of actually arriving at the end of the second millennium of Christian history, when the change of a date may literally cause all sorts of organisational problems in the routine workings of society, and possible disorder, because of the state of dependence on computer technology which has been reached. Governments concoct official celebration strategies to harness Millennium 'fever', as it is described – a mix of apprehension and diffused excitement – aiming to stabilise the status quo and rein in any forces for change. Millennial celebrations become a convenient marketing tool to promote competing nations, major cities and businesses in a global capitalist economy. What, then, can this mean for architecture?

It is worth just thinking back a thousand years, to put the coming of 2000 into some sort of perspective. The last millennium, which occurred during the early Middle Ages, ushered in a flowering of architecture in Europe, and a growth of urban centres, establishing what is seen as the real starting-point for the evolution of the practice and theory of architecture up until the present day, and on into the future. The reason for this spurt of creativity was the establishment of political stability, order and harmony between the secular and ecclesiastical powers in

Europe, with the coronation in 962 of Otto I as Holy Roman Emperor, and, in 999, the appointment of Gerbert of Aurillac, 'the most brilliant man of his day', as Pope Sylvester II. These conditions found eloquent architectural expression in the great number of churches, abbeys and cathedrals constructed.

The Benedictine abbey of Limburg was completed in 1042, and is widely regarded as marking the birth of the Romanesque: 'The importance of Limburg ... lies in the fact that the walls no longer merely confine space; they cease to be a flat, thin screen. By the use of piers, half-columns and pilaster strips ... component parts of the wall become a structural group which was in later experiments to support the overall vaulting of nave and side-aisles.' [1] In other words, the foundations for the development of the Gothic, and a whole new structural approach to architecture, had been laid, which, in the hands of the French, achieved an incredible level of refinement. 'Urbanisation, migration and warfare, political economy, art and architecture, religion and education, subtly intertwined to lay the foundation for the cultural supremacy of Paris for centuries to come, spearheading the general elan of urban revival in north-west Europe ...' [2]

It is interesting to consider whether there is any possibility that the architecture of the second millennium might achieve a comparable cultural significance. Certainly, the availability of funds for Millennium building projects suggests that there should be a flowering of architecture in the early years of the new century – including the major international projects such as Hanover and Sydney, as well as the new metropolitan monuments, and innumerable regional building initiatives. But the role of architecture in a globalised economy has become a rather particular one and, one might suggest, it manifests the privileging of style and aesthetics over content and social programme.

At a recent conference, Nigel Harris, from the Development Planning Unit at University College London, suggested that increased competition between countries and cities in a global economy, and the decentralisation of manufacturing, has led to a renewed emphasis on architecture and planning as a means of attracting inward investment to metropolitan areas. [3] He argues, 'the condition of the city is essential to profits.' For example, Mexico has become a huge provider of medical services to Americans at one-third of the price, while Cyprus has set up five English language universities to draw students from the Middle East Manila draws all the cartoons for Disney, and London has set itself up as a leader in the manufacture and delivery of 'culture'. But none of this can succeed if cities are deemed too unattractive, or unhygienic, or dangerous, by potential visitors. Harris points to the phenomenon of 'festivalisation' as an integral part of this process, whereby large-scale international events become essential elements in the pursuit of foreign visitors and investment, and cities compete ferociously for the privilege of hosting them.

Barcelona, for example, dramatically heightened its international public profile by the extensive programme of building and urban rehabilitation it undertook on the back of its selection to hold the 1992 Olympics, and the corresponding investment that was made in the city. Similarly, Atlanta, chosen to host the 1996 Olympics, used the event to launch a radical make-over of its image, which, until then, was defined by 'white flight' to the suburbs, and a deserted, decayed city centre – typical of many American cities. It is notable that the publicity machine for the Sydney Olympics in 2000 has chosen to focus on the fact that 'Sydney's $3.3 billion Olympic construction programme is ahead of Atlanta and Barcelona this far out from the Games. We have already let 95 per cent of the construction contracts' as a major publicity point. However, it can be argued that these types of 'festival' building programme are largely undertaken for the benefit of outsiders rather than city-dwellers, and they have been strongly criticised on this basis. Notwithstanding the fact that the RIBA chose to award its gold medal for architecture this year to the city of Barcelona for its achievements, geographer David Sibley has condemned the urban rehabilitation programme which the city council put in motion on the grounds of its social exclusionist intent and effect.[4] He has suggested that the design of new city squares and public places constituted a policy of removing dirt, the homeless and gypsies from the city centre before the Olympic visitors arrived, and suggested a parallel with Le Corbusier's Ville Radieuse plan for Paris, designed to impose order on a city which the architect viewed as 'a dangerous magma of human beings'. Similarly, anthropologist Charles Rutheiser levelled severe criticism at the highly corporatised Olympic construction programme for Atlanta, in his book *Imagineering Atlanta*.[5] He argues that 'the Olympic efforts of Atlanta's power structure have focused primarily on creating an appealing stage set for visitors and viewers ... a not so ingenious array of facades, props, smoke and mirrors designed to present the image of a healthy, vital and integrated city.' It featured a 'relentless use of advertising' and 'a minimum of new public investment and a maximisation of private profit'.

The Millennium offers an unparalleled 'festival opportunity' for cities, and many have jumped at the chance of justifying funding for some kind of eye-catching construction that will attract media attention, visitors and business. Essentially the architecture which has been commissioned by cities such as London, Paris, Hanover, Sydney, and even Beirut, Hong Kong and Tokyo – which do not subscribe to the Christian calendar and so have no genuine reason to celebrate the Millennium other than as a marketing opportunity and expression of economic alliance with other countries which do – is designed to make a visual impact, mainly through technical or structural virtuosity. Many of these structures have no other clear programme to do with function or content, and little specific connection with the reasons for celebrating the Millennium.

Neil Leach, in his recently published book, *Millennium Culture*,[6] is forthright in his definition of London's Millennium Dome as 'the perfect empty icon for rebranding London.' In fact he compares it with the Eiffel Tower in Paris, which, unsurprisingly, seems set to be repeated for the Millennium with the Tour de la Terre: 'It is in its depthlessness and its very emptiness of purpose that the Dome so closely echoes the Tower.' The main require-

ment is that it have an impressive exterior suggesting technical virtuosity.

One could say the same, perhaps, of the awe-inspiring Romanesque and Gothic cathedrals of the 11th and 12th centuries. Yet, at the turn of the second millennium, global society seems still to be in thrall to the excitement of technical achievement as an affirmation of humanity's control of its environment, while at the same time increasingly disturbed by the long-term ecological implications of the industrial and technological revolutions. This is manifested in the preference shown for High-Tech architecture when it comes to commissioning monuments for the Millennium – whether it be the Dome in London, or the Tour de la Terre in Paris with its nominal veneer of timber, or the 'Superdome' – going just one better – and Olympic Stadium at Sydney, the latter prompting comments from the public such as 'it is awesome', and 'I can't believe the expanse ... it is genuinely impressive.' Even in Beirut, a 10m Millennium Pavilion, commissioned by Solidere, the developers for the reconstruction of the city, to serve as a 'visitors' centre', has been designed by British High-Tech architect Nicholas Grimshaw (though the project is currently in abeyance). It is a typical, sophisticated, glazed box, held up by eye-catching structural 'trees', which was to have been illuminated with blue light at night to provide 'a unique modern icon for Beirut'. The exception to the rule is Japan's Communications Arch, designed by French architect Patrick Berger as an affirmation of Franco-Japanese economic friendship, made out of a monolithic block of Brittany granite apparently 'floating' above ground level. But though it may abjure the values of 'lightness' and transparency, and the habitual materials (glass and metal) of HighTech, this monument subscribes to the same agenda of visual impact and form over content as its millennial siblings.

The beauty of High-Tech for governments and business is that it provides an immediate visual expression of the impressive technological aspects of modern construction, and of high investment, while also giving every appearance of 'doing something' practical. Whatever the aesthetic potential of metal and glass and line privileged over plane, the essential victory is of pragmatism over poetry and the inexplicable, in line with the values of contemporary society. Since Richard Rogers and Renzo Piano first put the services on the outside of the Pompidou Centre, High-Tech architecture has been accepted as the solution to sophisticated and efficient servicing, suggesting a template for a type of 'active ecological systems' architecture which looks as if it is doing the job. In fact, as most people are aware, understated, passive low-tech is usually the more honest approach, and a blank mud-brick box, or an invisible, introverted courtyard building, the more environmentally responsive solution.

As we enter the third millennium, it is interesting to speculate how long this new generation of buildings, or constructions – so rapidly spawned as to allow scarcely a moment of consideration – will be with us. Certainly none of them will survive to see the next millennium, and few architects today would desire such longevity for their work, even in theory; but even the immediate future of these festival structures looks uncertain. Their real purpose is to provide a series of visual images which need not, and should not, perhaps, be constructed as buildings at all.

Notes

1 John Beckwith, *Early Medieval Art*, Thames and Hudson (London), 1983, p153.
2 Aidan Southall, *The City in Time and Space*, Cambridge University Press (Cambridge), 1998, p100–101.
3 Globalisation and World Cities: Reflections from Sao Paulo, conference held at the AA, May 1999.
4 Ibid.
5 Charles Rutheiser, *Imagineering Atlanta*, Verso (London), 1996.
5 Neil Leach, *Millennium Culture*, Ellipsis (London), 1999.

EXPO 2000, HANOVER

The world exposition that will be staged in Hanover next year exemplifies the primary themes and concerns which can be traced through the various 'Millennium projects' around the world. For Germany, it is a highly significant event, for, quite apart from the fact that the event coincides with the Millennium, it is the first time in the history of world expositions since the 19th century that one has been hosted on German soil. Moreover, it is the country's first major international event since the political unification of east and west.

The theme chosen for the Expo is Humankind–Nature–Technology, which is conveniently all-embracing for exhibitors, but also provides a focus for millennial anxiety about the relationship between man and his machines, and the well-documented, probably irreversible damage which they have caused to the natural environment since the Industrial Revolution. In this sense, the Expo is something of a curiosity: the first of its kind to acknowledge that it cannot be a simple, brash celebration of man's achievements, but must take on board a level of social and environmental responsibility – which is what one would expect from a country with Germany's track record, which includes the world's first ecological shopping centre, recently opened at Rommelmuhle, outside Stuttgart. The Expo organisers believe this is why the Bureau International des Expositions in Paris selected Hanover from the cities competing for the honour of hosting the Millennium Expo, although sadly the seriousness of intent is hardly communicated in the Expo mascot, Twipsy, designed by Javier Mariscal. This gormless object, which is supposed to 'put people in a marvellous mood', has one man's shoe, one woman's shoe, and a huge, mutated right hand raised in greeting, suggesting not so much welcome as uncertainty and insecurity about the human condition, much like the giant, genderless human figure designed for the Millennium Dome in London.

'My expectation is that we will be able to provide a platform for debates on solutions to the problems of the world and to the needs of humankind,' states Birgit Breuel, Commissioner General of Expo 2000, adding that, 'I also hope and expect that we will have a

Proposal for a pavilion from ZERI, Zero Emissions Research Initiative, (top), and MVRDV designed pavilion for the Netherlands (bottom).

Wilhelm Munthe-Kaas, LPO arkitektur & design, Oslo, are responsible for the Norwegian Pavilion (top right); Josef Wundt funded and designed the German Pavilion (centre); site plan of the exposition (bottom).

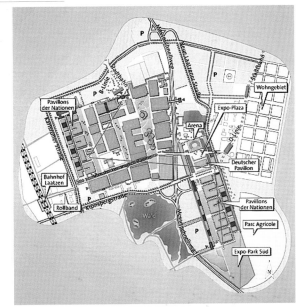

festival that is a lot of fun.' The Expo has been carefully designed to be neither an industrial fair nor an amusement park, while, obviously, generating a sense of excitement capable of attracting at least as many as the 42 million visitors to the Seville International World Expo of 1992, and plenty of business. Unlike Seville, where the re-use of the Expo site after the event was widely reported to be fraught with problems, the Hanover site makes use of the already existing Tradefair Grounds, which are being extended with the new 60-hectare Kronsberg site. This not only incorporates the Pavilion area and Expo Plaza, but also a business park, a 6000-home housing estate, and a new public park forming part of a green belt across the city. The layout is generated by the Expo concept of four 'pillars': the more than 170 nations and organisations from around the world who will be exhibiting in the pavilions; the 'Culture and Events' programme; another programme of 'Projects all over the World', aiming to take the ideas and benefits of the Expo to the places where they are really needed; and finally, the Thematic Area, the crucial focal point which will have a major role to play in attracting visitors and generating that essential sense of fun.

This area is essentially a series of 'spectacular' tableaux vivants installed in the existing Tradefair halls, extended with a new double-hall. Designed by Gerkan, Marg & Partners from Hamburg, it is fully glazed, with a self-supporting wooden roof and a pedestrian bridge connecting it to the Expo Plaza. The other architects invited include Jean Nouvel, responsible for Mobility and Future of Work, Toyo Ito, entrusted with Health, and a number of architects less well known internationally: Antoni Miralda (Nutrition), Ulrike Lauber and Wolfram Wohr (Energy), François Schuten (Future of the Past) and Rajeev Sethi (Basic Needs), plus the joint forces of the Creative Board (Humankind), and the Baden-Wurttemburg Film Academy (Environment: Landscape, Climate).

Inevitably, however, much of the serious architectural work at the Expo is being carried out by the ubiquitous big commercial practices: the Expo Plaza, including the pavilion of the Protestant and Catholic Churches of

Original proposal for the unrealised US Pavilion (top) by Frank Barlow/ Regine Leibinger, Berlin; Antti-Matti Siikala and Sarlotta Narjus, Finnish Pavilion (centre and bottom).

Germany, is by von Gerkan Marg, and the new railway station, connected by a sky-walk to the site, by Gossler and Düring. Although all buildings and infrastructure are supposed to conform to 'ecological' standards of design, it seems unlikely that they will demonstrate any radical revision of thought about design and construction after the Millennium. This is more likely to be found in the international pavilions, some of which are being designed by architects who have established strong reputations by challenging the status quo. The British pavilion design (on the theme 'No Man is an Island') is notably not among these, having been awarded for apparently political reasons to Goldbeck Bau Beiefeld, and featuring aluminium curtain walls; while Alsop and Störmer represents British architecture with a pavilion for Mercedes Benz. However, Japan has maintained its Expo patronage of experimental design with a giant construction made out of paper, designed by Shigeru Ban, and Peter Zumthor has designed for Switzerland a labyrinthine construction of stacked wooden beams held together by huge steel springs and bars, and devoid of contents. MVRDV has created for the Netherlands a 40m-high pavilion of five levels, each bearing a microcosm of a different type of Dutch landscape, with a floating roof supporting turbine windmills. Finland's pavilion, designed by Antti-Matti Slikala and Sarlotta Narjus, takes the form of a 'wind-nest', a mysterious box open to the sky and containing a small birch copse.

Many of the non-European countries have opted to construct pavilions which replicate or are based on traditional structures, many designed by German architects. The Holy See, too, with its terrible logo 'Jesus Christ – Yesterday, Today and Eternally', has commissioned a large German multidisciplinary firm and will have a large circular building of wood and glass. There is no getting away from the fact that, despite its ambitious environmental agenda, the primary focus of the Expo is political and economic, and Euro-centred.
Clare Melhuish

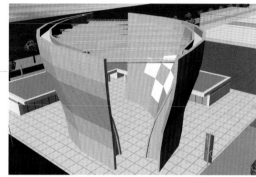

György Vadasz, Hungarian Pavilion (top and centre) and Republic of Korea's Pavilion (below) by Chul Kong, Kyong-Soo Park, Seoul.

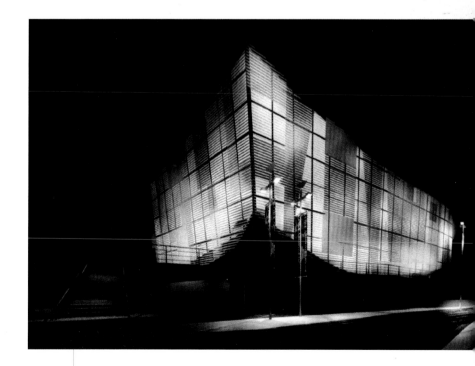

NICOLAS NORMIER
LA TOUR DE LA TERRE

The news that France had decided to celebrate the Millennium by building an apparently pointless wooden tower designed by a relatively unknown architect, Nicolas Normier, was greeted with some amusement in London, even though the concept of the supposedly functional Dome building was under severe attack, while plans for a comparably 'pointless' Millennium Ferris wheel on the Thames had received more positive, if low-key, support. The Tour de la Terre, like the wheel, is essentially a novelty, in a long tradition of French follies, including the Eiffel Tower of 1889 and Parc de la Villette of more recent times, with which it stands on axis, along the Canal de l'Ourcq. But the huge emphasis placed by the Mitterand regime on '*grands projets*' in the run-up to the Millennium seems to have exhausted the country's interest in constructing major buildings, at least for the time being.

The tower was to have been located next to one of those *grands projects*, the new national library by Dominique Perrault, a highly stylised design featuring four lofty glass towers of books, which were extensively criticised for being environmentally unsound. The 200m-high tower would have soared above the library towers, reducing them to a rather unflattering chimney-like appearance by comparison. The relocation of the tower could reasonably have been proposed because it symbolises an ecological agenda which embodies the criticism levelled at the library building. However that may be, the tower is now sited at some considerable distance east of Parc de la Villette, from which it can be reached by vaporetto along the canal.

The Tour de la Terre is thus named to express the dedication of the structure to all the cultures and civilisations of the world. The site on which it stands, measuring 18m in diameter, will be ritually offered as a piece of French soil to the world on 1 January 2000, when the President will declare its extra-territorial status – although the purpose of the tower, so far as it has one, will be very much to create another identifiable symbol for Paris. The choice of wood as a construction material is intended to celebrate the relationship between humankind and the earth, in response to the conclusions of the Earth Summit held in Rio de Janeiro – as expressed in a poetic statement issued by the architects:

'Au Monde, aux civilisations
Offrir une fleur à la terre
sera notre message
Construire en bois
notre hommage:
Hymne à la terre
et chant du monde.'

To the World, to civilisations,
to offer a flower to the earth
will be our message
To build in wood
Will be our homage
A hymn to the Earth
and a song of the world.

But, not unexpectedly, plans to use timber from five continents met with outrage from environmentalists. It is now intended to use glulam made from Scots fir to construct the eight trunks, each measuring 1.2m in diameter, which soar up to 'la grande fleur' high in the sky above. The use of glulam also seems questionable in environmental terms, as well as in terms of symbolic integrity, reducing the use of timber to something of a conceit, especially in view of the fact that the structure uses metal wind-bracing in conjunction with the trunks. The aim, however, is to create a distinct visual contrast to the all-metal structure of the Eiffel Tower which, at a time of rapid industrial growth, was regarded as embodying an ideal of modernity and progress. At the turn of the Millennium, the architects argue, 'the great revolution will lie in man's love for his environment,' which will be symbolised by the use of wood to construct the new tower.

The tower, however, is not supposed to be regarded simply as a symbolic structure, a sort of totempole for the 21st century. The fact that it also incorporates 2500m of usable space, between 80m and 100m above ground level, including a terrace-observatory, and accommodation for exhibitions, concerts, restaurants, radio transmission etc on four levels, is used to justify the structure in economic and rational terms – as indeed was the idea that the Eiffel Tower might be used as a research station for various purposes. As if to counter any suggestion that the prosaic character of the proposed functions may ultimately detract from the less material programme of the project, the architects propose that the metal and textile promenade spiralling around the outside of the structure will pass through 'a new timeless, celestial space'.

This hub of activity halfway up the tower is reached by panoramic lifts from its foot, as well as a metal staircase which winds its way up the inside of the trunk. The whole lower section of the tower is very much more streamlined than the Eiffel Tower, without any architectural or structural articulation of the meeting between the tower and the ground. But the design of the public facilities gives the tower the slightly disturbing appearance of being caught in a piece of airborne debris which has wrapped itself around the trunk, while the design of the five-petalled *grande fleur* at the top, each petal comprising a titanium frame against the sky, makes it look a little like an overgrown windmill.

Perhaps these aspects of the scheme are intentional, reinforcing as they do a form of anti-High-Tech visual aesthetic, which otherwise is contradicted by the spectacular nature of the evident technical achievement of building so high. The use of timber to create the impression of a 'natural' structure, combined with the close resemblance to a wind-turbine, gives some kind of earthy, visual expression to an 'ecological' agenda, in homage to Federico Mayor's affirmation at Rio in 1997 that 'The ethics of the future are those of the peasant.' Indeed, the tower will provide the focus for a new Cité de la Terre, or environmental centre, to be created at Bobigny, and a symbolic backdrop for the annual award of a newly created 'Prix de la Terre' which, along the lines of the Nobel Prize, will be presented to those selected for their particular environmental achievements, and bring Paris to prominence as a beacon for progress on environmental issues in the 21st century.
Clare Melhuish

SYDNEY OLYMPICS

The Sydney Olympics development at Homebush Bay has been very much driven by a high-profile ecological agenda, related to the pursuit of an image of distinct Australian identity in a global context. The site and the use of recycled water will be maximised within the Olympic development area. The Olympic Village at Newington is set to be the world's 'largest solar-powered suburb'. According to Maurice Strong, chairman of the Earth Council, the Games are set to be 'the greenest ... ever'.

The masterplan, designed by Hargreaves Associates, is based on an equal balance of built development and open parkland, containing numerous creeks and lakes, and sets out to establish a distinctively Australian landscape at the site. This intention has also informed the design of many of the buildings, by a diverse array of architects, although the major Olympic landmarks, including the Stadium and Superdome, conform to a predominantly international High-Tech aesthetic, affirming structural and functional efficiency.

Stadium Australia was designed by the UK's stadia specialists, Lobb Partnership, in a joint venture with Australian practice Bligh Voller Nield, and the explicit intention was to set a new benchmark for stadia around the world. The hyperbolic paraboloid structure of the roof allowed the construction of huge spans, which in turn allow a very high level of flexibility of use.

The Superdome, which will accommodate concerts as well as sporting events, has been designed by one of Australia's biggest architectural practices, Cox Richardson, with US sports consultants Devine de Flon Yaeger. It has a steel-framed roof supported by tension cables from masts around the outer perimeter of the seating bowl, forming what the architects describe as a 'coronet of slender steel elements'. But it also features a 70kw photovoltaic power plant which is the largest solar rooftop system in Australia, and will allow the building to have 'near zero green house effect'.

One particular aspect of the Superdome design has been hailed as distinctively 'Australian' in character, and that is the way the grand foyer wraps around the building 'as a typical Australian verandah', with its roof suspended from the external mast structure. This fits in with the guidelines on Australian architectural style offered by the Urban Design Review Panel which was formed in 1996 to act in an advisory capacity to the Olympic Coordination Authority. Chairman Chris Johnson defines its essence as an 'open-ended' treatment of space, in contrast to the customary enclosure of space in European architectural tradition: 'It's about people moving through and passing to places – it's much more dynamic', he says. 'It's reminiscent of Australian country towns with wide main streets flanked by long shady verandahs.'

This conception of space and architecture underlies the masterplan layout, with a broad,

The High-Tech of the Stadium Australia (opposite) and the Superdome – Sydney Olympics' landmark buildings – contrasts with the simplicity and geometric clarity of buildings such as the Sydney International Shooting Centre (top), Archery Park (centre) and Olympic Park Station (bottom).

tree-lined, open-ended Olympic Boulevard at its heart, on either side of which the main sports buildings and the showground and exhibition complex are assembled. From this central spine, and associated Fig Tree Grove, 'green fingers' of open space reach out to connect with the parkland and wetland expanses, designed by a number of different landscape architecture practices and encircling the Olympic development from the northwest to the southern sides.

All the buildings on the site, and at the other associated sites dispersed around Sydney, subscribe to an aesthetic of simplicity and geometric clarity which on the one hand is typical of international event architecture, but may also be read as an interpretation of an indigenous architectural form which has evolved in response to a predominantly outdoor, pioneering lifestyle, where construction was a matter of practicality and making use of readily available materials. For example, the buildings of the International Equestrian Centre at Horsley Park, by EQUUS 2000, refer to 'simple Australian "shed" architecture', while the International Shooting Centre at Cecil Park, by Group GSA Architects, is designed as 'a truly "Australian" response ... to the natural contour and landform', generating 'a simple industrial roof and mass'. The Finish Tower at the International Regatta Centre, Penrith Lakes, by Conybeare Morrison is, likewise, 'derived from the rural look of hardy steel-clad farm buildings, but with a refinement befitting an Olympic venue'.

Visually, then, the architecture of the Sydney Olympics will be distinguished by a primarily horizontal expanse of well-articulated roof and canopy structures, expressing a strong local interest in defining an aesthetic of shelter which abjures the fanciful and decorative in architectural terms, interacts with the landscape setting, and gives a flavour of an Australian vernacular. The Olympic Park Station, designed by Hassell, which connects the heart of the Homebush Bay site to the centre of Sydney, exemplifies the terms of this architecture as a broad, linear, open-ended canopy structure stretched over a series of structural arches.

The interest in dome design represents an extension of this over-arching roof concept. It is seen not only in its ubiquitous, millennial High-Tech form, with the use of prominent external structural masts, but also in a contrasting 'natural' version using laminated timber ribs, as over the main hall in the Exhibition Complex, by Ancher Mortlock Woolley. Ken Woolley suggests, 'There's something about the completeness of a dome that makes it a very powerful image': a fitting comment, perhaps, on the collection of architectural projects from around the world which will usher in the third millennium.
Clare Melhuish

EDWIN HEATHCOTE
EXPRESSIONISM VERSUS FUNCTIONALISM: THE BATTLE FOR THE SOUL OF THE MILLENNIAL CHURCH

As a preface to his project descriptions of three Millennium churches, Edwin Heathcote describes how functionalism and Expressionism have dominated church design throughout the 20th century. Perhaps a swan song to the sacred.

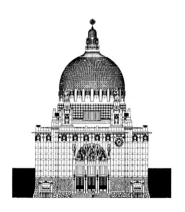

Otto Wagner, Steinhof Church, Vienna.

If it was Nietzsche who declared that God was dead, it was Otto Wagner who created the architectural epitaph with his Kirche am Steinhof. Building began in 1907, the year in which Einstein published his Special Theory of Relativity which introduced a new era in the understanding and questioning of time, space and man's place in the cosmos. Created as the chapel for a mental asylum on the outskirts of Vienna, the city where Freud was working on theories which would augur changes in Western mankind's self-perception even more dramatic than those of Einstein, this was that greatest of paradoxes: a Functionalist church. I say that the Functionalist church is a paradox, if not an oxymoron, as it is a place of blind faith in the irrational. A church can be functional in that it accommodates the brief of ritual, procession and accommodation, but beyond this is a blur. Wagner's building, based on a Greek cross plan, was designed with wide aisles so that patients having a fit could be efficiently removed; relatives of the ill were accommodated in galleries and the stoup consisted of a fountain of running holy water, a device to stop infection spreading from patient to patient. White, bright and light with a slightly raked floor so that all participants could see the altar clearly, this was a consummate Modernist building. Nevertheless it retained the traditional symbolic elements, the dome of the heavens surmounting the crossing, the cruciform plan and a full complement of Secessionist fittings to make the church a fine example of both Otto and Richard Wagner's notion of the total work of art: the *Gesamtkunstwerk*. This is a church by a rationalist, a non-believer who was able to reassess the church not as a mystical container of numinosity but as a functional building. It laid the foundations for a rationalisation of church architecture.

Three years earlier William Lethaby had produced his masterpiece, the Church of All Saints at Brockhampton. Like Wagner, he too saw the church in functional terms but his building was very different to Wagner's. He embraced structural advances (using a concrete roof, albeit thatched) but at the same time referred heavily to historical forms and symbolism and local vernacular. His church with its pointy, triangular arches (echoing the metaphor of the church as tent of God) ushered in a kind of moody Expressionism based on archetypal associations, deep shadows, radically yet deceptively simple spaces and Platonic forms. Despite his functional assertions, the church became a lucid appendix to his book, *Architecture, Mysticism and Myth* in which he looked at building as a manifestation of being speaking through a Jungian collective subconscious and the recognition of meaningful forms.

In these two buildings I believe we have the seeds of the two strains of ecclesiastical architecture which have defined developments in the best churches of the 20th century and which continue to dominate advances in the field. Those two trends, which are not necessarily mutually exclusive, can be broadly described as Functionalism and Expressionism.

Functionalism descends in a direct line from Wagner; he analysed the brief for a church in the same way he did that for the Post Office Savings Bank at around the same time. Wagner's architectural rationalisation presaged moves for liturgical reform from progressive elements within the Church. From around the turn of the century there were increasing demands to reassess ecclesiastical architecture and move away from the traditional separation of clergy and laity and the deliberate mystification of the ritual. These changes were expressed in ideas about the democratisation of space and an emphasis on clarity and unity in church design as well as the use of new technologies to provide well-lit interiors with rational, unobtrusive structures.

Frank Lloyd Wright, working at the same time as Lethaby and Wagner, pioneered this rationalisation in his blocky Unity Chapel in Oak Park, Illinois (1906), a concrete cube of American democratic space. At Notre Dame du Raincy (1922) Auguste Perret used the structural strength of concrete to realise the Gothic dream of diaphanous walls which melt away into light and the creation of a unified single space unhindered by massive columns. Otto Bartning's Seel Church, Essen (1928) was the manifestation of a further simplification of ecclesiastical design, its stark, industrial steel structure allowing translucent glass walls and a completely unified space. Rudolf Schwarz's Church of Corpus Christi at Aachen (1930) attained a sublime level of purity in a design that would now probably be termed Minimalist; a white box, brilliantly lit with a simple open bell-tower, the ultimate in reductivism.

Frankly, neither of these latter two churches has been bettered by 'more modern' structures, in the same way that Le Corbusier's villas remain paradigms of modern architecture. There have, however, been notable efforts; Mangiarotti and Morasutti's church

Christian Kerez, Chapel in the mountains at Oberrealta, 1992-93.

John and Heikki Siren, Ottaniemi Chapel, Finland, 1957.

Tadao Ando, Church on the Water, Tonamu, Japan, 1988.

in Baranzate, Milan (1958) is a kind of Japanese-influenced version of Perret's church, its diaphanous walls translated into translucent glazed panels which echo paper screens stretched on a delicate framework of steel. Gunnar Asplund's Woodland Crematorium (Stockholm, 1940) used the primeval power of the landscape to create a Classical temple for the Modernist age while Kaija and Heikki Siren built another reductivist homage to the landscape in their Otaniemi Chapel (Finland, 1957) where a wall slides open to reveal a simple cross set against the pine trees, very much in the manner of Caspar David Friedrich's Romantic visions.

Swiss architect Christian Kerez has contributed to this sophisticated Minimalism set against the background of romantic nature with two tiny buildings: the mortuary chapel at Bonaduz (1992–93) and a chapel in the mountains at Oberrealta (also 1992–93). The first of these can be seen as a kind of paean to the symbolism of the burial mound, the most archetypal of pagan images, while the second is a version of the mountain shrines which dot the Alps, a homage to the tradition of the grotto and the notion of creating the sacred within the landscape, a device to help the superstitious, lonely traveller on his way. Both these structures reinterpret archetypal forms in a truly modern manner using a sparse, yet poignant, minimal vocabulary.

This vein of poetic Functionalism (often combined with vague pantheistic leanings) has also survived in the work of Tadao Ando and others. Ando's Church on the Water (Tonamu, Japan, 1988) is a pure development of the Sirens' chapel, revelling in its backdrop of nature, while his Church of the Light (Ibraki, Japan 1989) burns a brilliant cross of light on to the retinas of its congregation. The Functionalist tradition is also evident in Juha Leiviska's Church of St John (Männistö, Finland, 1992) and Myräkki Church (Vantaa, Finland, 1984) where the architect tempers spatial inventiveness with a brilliant purity held together in a sophisticated framework of intersecting planes and surfaces reminiscent of De Stijl.

The other trend which has defined avant-garde developments in 20th-century church architecture is Expressionism. Insepara-

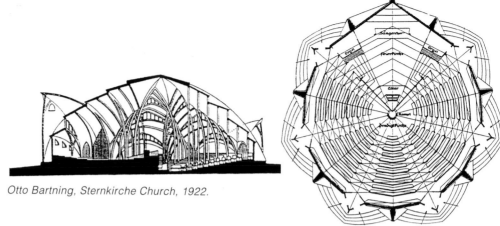

Otto Bartning, Sternkirche Church, 1922.

The Bauhaus manifesto, 1919.

ble from the roots of Modernism, Expressionism emerged as a force in Germany around the period of the First World War and built on the dynamism and movement of Art Nouveau and Symbolism. The extent to which the genesis of both the Modern Movement and Expressionism were interconnected can be seen in the early works which emerged from the Bauhaus. The manifesto (1919) appeared with a titlepage designed by Lyonel Feininger depicting a sparkling, abstracted Gothic church, the 'Cathedral of Socialism', revealing the roots of the Bauhaus ideal in the medieval guild tradition, with the *Gesamtkunstwerk* of the Gothic cathedral as its model. The spirit of the Gothic pervaded the spiky forms and deep shadows of Expressionism and melded with crystalline and geological forms to create a new vein of architecture which was perfectly suited to sacred buildings; a deep (if vague) mysticism ran through the thought of the early Modernists.

Otto Bartning was at the forefront of this adaptation of Expressionist forms into ecclesiastical design. His Sternkirche design of 1922 represented a remarkable leap forward in thinking, one of the first truly modern visions of a church which blended contemporary architecture with liturgical innovations; the socialist ideals of the architects who followed him coincided neatly with the radical democratisation of space and the emphasis on the community which characterised avant-garde thinking in the Church at this time. The churches of Dominikus Böhm, Rudolf Schwarz, Clemens Holzmeister and Fritz Hëger, although little known, represent certainly the most radical advances made in ecclesiastical design during the twentieth century. This powerful vein of Germanic Expressionism continued after the Second World War, but during the postwar period the church which has attracted the most attention is undoubtedly Le Corbusier's Notre Dame du Haut, Ronchamp (1950–54). Corbusier's church blurs the line between Functionalism and Expressionism just as the line was blurred by the mystical idealism of the early Bauhaus. But, coming exactly in the middle of the twentieth century it also presented the world of ecclesiastical architecture with a crisis which has not since been resolved.

An atheist and arch Functionalist, when Le Corbusier was called on to create a sacred building he made what he believed to be a sacred space. There is no real analysis of the brief; Ronchamp, impressive though it may be, is wilful; an abstract sculpture. Some may argue that Corb was a genius with a Midas touch and the architectural equivalent of papal infallibility but,

whether we like Ronchamp or not, it was a disaster for church architecture because it was taken by architects around the world as the cue for church buildings to become a kind of safety valve for repressed artists. Frustrated architects churning out non-bourgeois social housing and other machines-for-living-in were suddenly given licence to let loose if they were ever commissioned to design a church. Expressionism became OK. The result was thousands of ill-conceived and empty architectural gestures. This attitude has persisted and contaminated most contemporary church design.

On the other hand a vein of contemporary Expressionism has survived which can be traced back to the original German and Central European experiments. Of all these perhaps Hungarian architect Imre Makovecz's work is the most remarkable. His brand of highly personal Expressionism blends the metamorphic, organic forms of Rudolf Steiner with a kind of pagan architectural symbolism which is deeply affecting and startlingly original. At his best, in the church at Paks (1987) for instance, he achieves one of the most memorable twentieth-century spaces: a sprouting nave with a structure which seems to be shooting upwards, a scaley, organic spire, a bulging zoomorphic body and a forcefully sexual entrance sequence. The mix of organic, sexual and mythical imagery creates a profound impression and presents a millennial vision which runs deliberately counter to the aesthetics of Functionalism.

Fay Jones' roots lie with Frank Lloyd Wright and the Prairie School and his work too owes something to the Gothic and something to an Expressionist vision. His Mildred B Cooper Memorial Chapel (Arkansas, 1988) and Thorncrown Chapel (Arkansas, 1981) create new interpretations of the idea of the temple as a clearing in the forest, structure as the sheltering branches of trees. Santiago Calatrava used a more High-Tech version of a similar image in his visionary design for a bioshelter for New York's Cathedral of St John the Divine (1991) is in an organic/Gothic/High-Tech vein which stems from Viollet-le-Duc and embraces Gaudí and Horta along the way.

If the Functionalist and the Expressionist can be separated out in this way and traced back to their antecedents, there is also a more problematic vein which falls between the two – the gap can be unfortunately deep. Recent years have seen revivals of aesthetics first propounded by Cubists and later Expressionists. The former found architectural expression in the crystalline work of the Czech Cubist architects while the latter revolves around

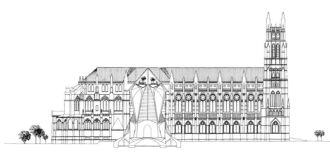

Santiago Calatrava, Cathedral of St John the Divine, New York, 1991.

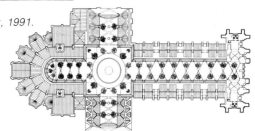

Imre Makovecz, Church at Paks, 1987.

both the architectural and filmic oeuvres of Germany's Weimar Republic. Both movements were obsessed with geological forms; inspired by Einstein's new theories about the relativity of time and space, crystalline formations were looked on as the embodiment of both mass and the vastness of geological time, four dimensions captured in a fragmented nugget of Existential affirmation.

Philip Johnson, the greatest of self-confessed architectural whores, has, as usual, led the way in a new trend with his plans for the Cathedral of Hope, Dallas, Texas (1996) with a great jagged rock of a building while his Crystal Cathedral (Garden Grove, California) of 1980 is a Las Vegas-vulgar version of the Expressionist dream of the cosmic mountain of glass, a vision expressed by Paul Scheerbart in his 'Glass Architecture' of 1914. The star-shaped plan and gleaming glass spire of the church stem directly from the images of the mystical side of early Modernism. The interior of Matti Sanaksenho's design for a chapel in Turku, Finland (1995) is reminiscent of the pointed arches of the 1920s churches of Dominikus Böhm, and of Lethaby's Brockhampton before that.

This leaves us in a position at the beginning of the new millennium not too dissimilar from that of 100 years ago. We have architectural pluralism but the sense of direction felt by Wagner and Lethaby is distinctly lacking. Both these proto-Functionalists were working (from more or less opposite directions) towards a common goal of the modern, rational city. They were building in an age where faith was beginning to collapse but was still essentially strong and remained at the heart of Western society. A little less than a century later we are in an age of 'weak faith' or post-Christianity. Rudolf Schwarz, probably the most influential theorist of ecclesiastical architectural renewal, wrote in 1938:

It does not suffice to work honestly with the means and forms of our own time. It is only out of sacred reality that sacred building can grow. What begets sacred works is not the life of the world but the life of faith – the faith, however, of our own time ... that sacred substance out of which churches can be built must be alive and real to us. (*Bau der Kirche*, Lambert Schneider, Heidelberg, 1938, translated 1958 as *The Church Incarnate*, pp8–9)

The problem seems to be, as Charles Jencks indicates elsewhere in this book, that faith has virtually evaporated, even within the Church. Once faith (or rather conviction) has collapsed the only routes to exploring ecclesiastical architecture are personal Expressionism or rational examination of the brief to create a purely functional building. Neither option on its own is generally satisfactory. We are left with a series of architectural gestures and generalisations. The communities in which new churches are built are rarely consulted, and without this gesture the buildings cannot succeed on Rudolf Schwarz's terms or as the heart of a new community. Most churches are built around a vague notion of the sacred, repeated clichés (crosses cut out of walls, spires, massive walls with slit-like openings, expressionistic roofs etc). The general impression of ecclesiastical architecture at the close of the 20th century is that most architects are not sure quite what to do. Many want to design a church, it still retains a certain caché and prestige as a building type, but as they're not quite sure what goes on inside (apart from what is in the brief), it becomes an exercise akin to designing a new art gallery. In fact I would say that the art gallery has become the twentieth century equivalent of ecclesiastical space; the church has unfortunately fallen by the wayside as an expression of the *Zeitgeist*. At the turn of the last millennium, afraid the world would end in the year 1000, the new millennium bringing with it the Last Judgement, Christians fell back on their pagan roots and began to worship idols. By now these idols had taken the form of relics. People attempted to touch these symbols of holiness, to benefit from their aura by being near them. They paid to be buried near relics (which is why old churches are full of bodies) as they believed some of this holiness would rub off on their corpses. These relics became the anchors of the church and objects of pilgrimage. Now people spend their Sunday afternoons (sometimes their holidays) going to art galleries. The relics which hang there are held in equal reverence and awe. They are worth a fortune, guarded, placed jewel-like in temples to artistic genius. Everyone believes in art. The museum has become a kind of Holy Grail to architects, the most prestigious buildingtype, often coming with a huge budget. The church is left as a kind of oddity. Too few architects are left examining the question of sacred architecture in a serious way (regardless of whether they are Christian or not); weak faith has led to weak architecture. Despite a few excellent designs along the way, the architectural promises of Wagner, Lethaby and Gaudí, the first Functionalists and the first Expressionists, have not been fulfilled. Yet it is these architects from the dawn of the 20th century, and those who came in their immediate wake, whose work remains the foundation for modern church architecture as it moves into the next century.

RICHARD MEIER
CHURCH FOR THE YEAR 2000, ROME

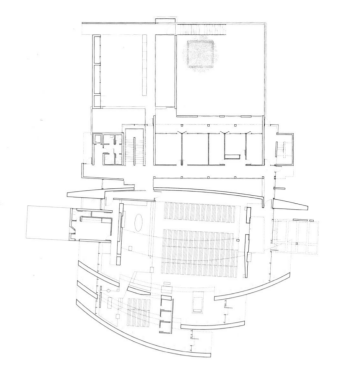

Pope John Paul II has proclaimed the year 2000 to be a Holy Year and to mark this special event, the Vicariato di Roma has embarked on an ambitious programme to build 50 new churches in and around Rome. Most of these were to be built in the deprived suburbs of the city, districts which had grown quickly and lacked churches; it was a gesture from a particularly evangelic Vatican which had appeared to be ignoring the rapidly expanding city on its doorstep. The most important of these new churches was to be that in the Tor Tre Teste district. An initial open architectural competition produced no clear winner and a new, limited competition was launched. The six architects asked to submit designs read like a *Who's Who* of the most influential late 20th century architects: Tadao Ando, Günter Behnisch, Santiago Calatrava, Peter Eisenman, Frank O Gehry and Richard Meier. None of these architects is known particularly for their ecclesiastical work and in fact only Tadao Ando has built any churches of note. Neither was the religious background of the architects deemed important. The resulting designs made for a good exhibition; a fine collection of

individual monuments encapsulating the architects' distinctive approaches and they must have reflected well on the informed good taste of the committee. In 1996, Richard Meier was announced as the winner. Meier's only previous involvement in sacred architecture had been his design for the Hartford Seminary, Connecticut (1978–81). Meier (along with Eisenman) had been one of the 'Whites', the group of architects that resurrected purist Modernism from the ashes of Po-Mo excess. Tom Wolfe placed Meier firmly in the 'Scholastics' chapter of *From Bauhaus to Our House*. It is no surprise, then, that his winning design should be white. Generated by subtle geometries and the slight dislocation of the church within a grid set up by the support buildings, Meier has created an intriguing plan.

Like many architects before him, Meier has used the heavily symbolic geometries of the square and the circle to organise the building. The plan of the church has been generated by segments of a circle in much the same way as Utzon used segments of a sphere for the Sydney Opera House and Libeskind did in his design for the Imperial War Museum North. The circle is taken to represent perfection, the dome of the heavens and, ultimately, God. The solidity of the square represents the earth, the four elements and the rational intellect. Libeskind has proposed using segments of a fragmented sphere to create an image of a fractured world, a Humpty-Dumpty globe smashed by war and tragedy, impossible to reassemble. Meier has attempted to use similar symbolism to express the unity of the church and the numinosity of sacred space. On plan it becomes clear that Meier has adopted this device in an effort to reach out to

the community, a kind of scoop to gather together the lost sheep of this dreary and deprived suburb. It is the image of a hand reaching out to help. It is also reminiscent of a bunch of bananas. The three concrete shells which emerge from the plan create the body of the nave together with a spine wall that is skewed slightly from the simple geometry of the surrounding buildings which embrace community halls and meditation spaces. The three curved elements are meant to represent the Holy Trinity while a reflecting pool highlights the role of the ritual of baptism. The form of the building is undoubtedly both sculptural and striking and the new church will become a major landmark and a place of architectural, if not Christian, pilgrimage.

Meier has built his impressive reputation on a series of museums and major buildings whose forms are generated by the internal functions and the external urban and site conditions, building up a series of layers, sometimes subtly fragmented and disconnected, at other times exquistely engineered and illuminated in a rigid Modernist grid. Driven by function, Meier inherits the mantle of the Bauhaus. Ecclesiastical architecture, however, is notoriously difficult to pare down to forms following functions. Churches are the built expression of faith and ritual. Faith is intangible and tends to become the excuse for wilful Expressionist gestures which repressed Modernists need to get out of their systems (*pace* Ronchamp). But ritual can be defined in terms of function. The early years of Modernism coincided exactly with dramatic reforms in Christian thinking on the liturgy. The Christian Churches saw a move away from the separation of clergy from laity, and the democratisation of the internal space of the church. Just as Modernist ideas were based around social revolution and the formation of a utopian, egalitarian society (its evangelists were the agit-prop constructivists and the Bauhaus) so the changes in liturgical thinking reflected a move towards the importance of the congregation as a corporate body coming together within a building stripped of its mystical roots. The Church moved towards the idea of community centre and Meier has certainly addressed this aspect of church through his provision of extensive public facilities. Where he seems to have failed, however, is within the form of the church itself.

We can use the dramatic changes which occurred in twentieth-century theatre design as a guide to the upheavals in Modernism in ecclesiastical architecture. In the nineteenth century the audience and the actors were distinctly separated by the proscenium arch. In the twentieth century designers began to move away from this separation (partly as a response to cinema which introduced the separation of the screen) and to bring the actors closer to the audience with thrust stages and theatres in the round. This is a helpful analogy as church design developed in broadly the same direction; the barriers (let us say the rood screen or the separation of the sanctuary from the nave) between congregation and clergy were removed. Meier's church is a nineteenth-century theatre with the audience on one side and the actors on the other; from a religious point of view it does not acknowledge these changes in liturgical thinking. Thus, it cannot be a modern building, no matter what it looks like. The light from the windows behind the altar will be dazzling with the setting sun behind them, the congregation will not be able to see. The church is entered from the east rather than the traditional west, and while this is understandable from an urbanistic point of view (it allows

the building to open up towards the housing projects), it represents another abandonment of the symbolic role of the church. Meier has adopted a pick-and-mix symbolism, incorporating those bits which suit his work and discarding others. Finally, this building is the paradigm of an architectural *fait accompli*. One of the reasons for the failure of these suburban housing projects has traditionally been that they were imposed on their inhabitants from above, communities played no part in their planning. The church is the spiritual home of the community and the very notion of constructing 50 new ones at this time is to provide a heart for deprived and soulless suburbs; to use these buildings as tools for the reintegration of the disenfranchised poor. While the problems with Meier's church have as much to do with the brief as with the architect, it is illustrative of the unsatisfactory nature of imposing a church on a community without consultation and by competition. This building may well become a landmark for architects, a thoughtful piece of urban design and a powerful public sculpture for Tor Tre Teste, but it may have already failed to become the metaphysical shelter for the soul of the district's deprived inhabitants.
Edwin Heathcote

RAFAEL MONEO
OUR LADY OF THE ANGELS CATHEDRAL

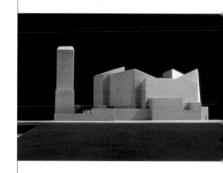

Of the three major Millennium churches which we are looking at here, Moneo's new cathedral for the 'city of angels' is paradoxically both the most traditional and the most adventurous. In essence the plan is cruciform; a long nave, a crossing and transepts. All walls of the building flare towards the crossing and the altar, and the roof rises towards the east end. Moneo, unlike Meier in his Church for the Year 2000 in Rome, decided to retain the traditional orientation with the apse facing east. Yet the site did not lend itself to this orientation as the plaza created before it is on towards the east of the site necessitating entrances on the church's east end, ie behind the altar. To overcome this anomaly the architect has created ambulatories which take the visitor along passages on either side of the nave until the cathedral is entered from the west side at the end of this walk, or at other points along the nave. This has led to a curious inversion of the accustomed plan whereby the side chapels inhabit the spaces to either side of the nave; here the congregation walks past the chapels (which face towards the ambulatories, away from the nave) on the way into the cathedral. This gives a highly unusual sense of pilgrimage and journey on the passage into the building.

Although this presents an unconventional interpretation of the traditional entrance and orientation it also has the effect of knitting the sacred and the profane realms together in an effective and inviting manner. The word 'profane' in fact derives from the Latin *pro fanum* – in front of the temple – and Moneo has created two new spaces: that inside the church and that of the plaza outside which is capable of becoming an outdoor church.

The building is positioned downtown in a city which has difficulty with the very notion of a downtown. The orientation towards the automobile has stripped Hollywood of a coherent urban centre and one of the primary intentions of the architect in the design of the site was to engender an urban approach to it within the disparate setting alongside Hollywood Freeway and bounded by Hill Street, Grand Street and Temple Street. The cathedral became the focus of a development which embraces the Cardinal's Residence, Parish Center and a public plaza as well as car parking. The architect compares this self-contained development to the 'missions' erected by the Franciscan Order. The cathedral, placed at the higher end of a significantly sloping site, remains the dominant element within the composition and the freestanding

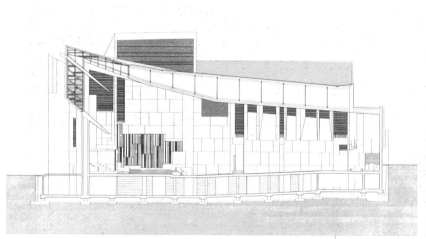

Longitudinal section

campanile becomes the billboard, announcing the presence of the cathedral to the freeway at the apex of the site. Covered walkways to either side of the huge plaza at the heart of the complex introduce the monastic device of the cloister and help to define the routes into the church. The cathedral's dramatic, although minimal, west elevation becomes the backdrop for outdoor ceremonies to be held within the plaza. The focus of this facade is the enormous, theatrical cross defined in negative cut through an alabaster skylight. Illuminated from within at night, this will become a less than subtle signpost, easily competing with the city's neons.

This same cross is the culmination of the building's interior. Set behind the altar, the cross consists of the transom and mullion subdividing the single great alabaster light. The transom and sill have expansive surfaces which angle down towards the nave, directing light towards the congregation. The fact that the light is filtered through translucent alabaster means that this will not be a blinding beam of sun – it is a less didactic symbol than Ando's cross of light (which is the converse of this window) at his Church of the Light, Ibaraki, Osaka. The rest of the light is provided by clerestoreys above the side chapels. The chapels (opening not into the nave but on to the ambulatories) are defined within irregularly spaced dense piers which create a sculptural configuration at the sides of the nave and give the effect of enormously thick walls. There are distinct echoes in the plan of Le Corbusier's tapering slit-like openings at Ronchamp but the effect here is altogether different, lacking the wilful Expressionism of Corb's revered church and lightening the sense of containment by creating the wall from a series of independent enclosures.

Moneo's church manages an unusual feat; while retaining a cruciform plan and the traditional orientation, he has created a building which is an innovative modern interpretation of the changes addressed in Vatican II within a recognised architectural iconography. The notion (expressed in Vatican II) that the clergy and laity be brought together in one great communion, the barriers between them brought down while the church was to become merely the shelter for the ritual and not to draw attention to itself as monument or distraction, made most of the great ecclesiastical buildings liturgically redundant at a single stroke. The new cathedrals which followed these dictates may have answered these reforms but they often failed to connect with people's notion of what a church should be – the church

is, after all, probably the most profound architectural archetype in Western civilisation. Some small churches managed successfully to engender the required spirit of modesty, community and elegant beauty but the architects of larger churches and cathedrals in particular, have been signally unsuccessful in their search for a new form language. One of the main problems has been the adoption of platonic or simplistic forms – cubes, tee-pees, cones, etc. In employing the cruciform plan but using the transepts as seating brought close to the altar (rather than filling the transepts with the more traditional sidechapels), Moneo has achieved an effect close to that of theatre in the round or, perhaps more accurately, thrust stage, which has brought the worshippers to the heart of the action.

The gestures which the new cathedral makes towards the city are spatial rather than aesthetic. Like the basilicas of the early Christians this is a building which gives little away to the outside. Its exterior is robust, its form expressed in a mixture of concrete, stone, alabaster, wood and bronze. To me it suggests a concert hall or theatre, some public building for performance (its sophisticated but tough section reminds me of the work of Hans Scharoun); there is nothing precious or attention-seeking on the outside. Instead the focus is the interior; and it is by the use of space and light that Moneo creates a sense of the numinous, not with art or artifice. By introducing a more complex form language which is both radical in its architecture yet closely related to existing typologies, Moneo has succeeded in pulling off the clever trick of seemingly covering all the angles.
Edwin Heathcote

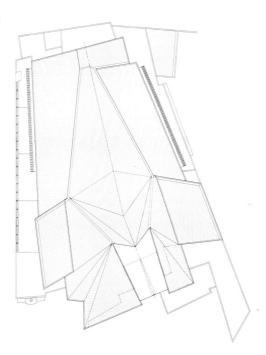

Roof plan

RENZO PIANO

PADRE PIO PILGRIMAGE CHURCH

San Giovanni Rotondo

The largest modern church in Europe is taking shape in an Italian village in the deprived region of Puglia in an extraordinary gesture to mark the life of one of Christanity's most enigmatic figures of recent years. Renzo Piano had originally refused the commission to build a pilgrimage church dedicated to the holy man Padre Pio, but, after great encouragement from the head of the San Giovanni Rotondo Capuchin Order, he was finally persuaded to take it on. The brief, to create a building to house over 7000 worshippers, is almost unprecedented. It is an enormous undertaking and testimony to the incredible growth of the cult around Padre Pio, the monk who will be reburied in the church's crypt and to whom the building is dedicated.

Padre Pio (1887–1968), a pious, ascetic and fanatical Catholic, became a friar at San Giovanni Rotondo and in 1918 apparently developed stigmata after a fearful dream or vision whilst in a trance. The reputation of this miraculous holy man snowballed into a cult and during his lifetime he became a near saint. Disturbed by his influence, the Vatican ordered that he say Mass in private only and that he limit his activities and pronouncements. He subsequently covered his 'stigmata' with mittens and avoided the great crowds that fought to touch him in hope that some of his sanctity would rub off on them. He was associated with a number of 'miracles' including the healing of a woman close to the priest who later became Pope John Paul II. The latter subsequently assiduously advanced the cause of Padre Pio who is widely expected to be canonised in the Holy Year 2000. The community hopes that the new church will be completed in time for the canonisation of the little village's most famous set of remains. The cult surrounding relics and the popularity of pilgrimages which stems from it, dates from around the millennial angst which engulfed Europe 1000 years ago. In an atmosphere where it was widely believed that the world would end and judgement would come (which coincided with widespread crop failures and famine) worshippers turned towards relics to be close to holiness and thus personal salvation. Some thousand years later it is difficult not to see parallels.

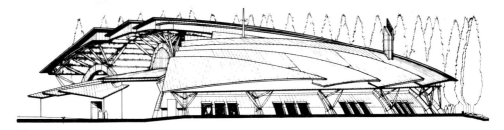

With a brief demanding a capacity for 7200 pilgrims (plus a further 30,000 outside the building), Piano's pilgrimage church is hardly a conventional place of worship and it would be wrong to criticise it using the criteria which would normally be applied to a more modest church. The building is between church and stadium and its genesis is indebted equally to the development of both these building types. Piano's new building can be usefully compared to Pierre Vago's St Pius X Basilica at Lourdes, France (1958) which required a similarly enormous capacity. Confronted with the problem of how to place such a gargantuan structure (a shelter for up to 22,000) into the picturesque French landscape without exerting an elephantine presence, Vago decided to bury the structure so that only a huge turfed ellipse is visible above ground. Apart from this obvious difference, Piano's new building and Vago's basilica have much in common. In both the mind of the master engineer is evident; Vago had assistance from Eugene Freyssinet, who had pioneered the use of pre-stressed concrete in engineering, while Piano collaborated with the late Peter Rice in the early stages of the design. Both structures are designed with shallow concave floors to increase visibility and awareness of the sheer mass of people so that the congregation becomes the spectacle. Both architects have used the curve as opposed to the straight line in an effort to embrace the mass of pilgrims and to ensure no one feels stuck in a corner, far from the action. Architecturally, however, Piano's structure, although smaller, is the more adventurous of the two designs.

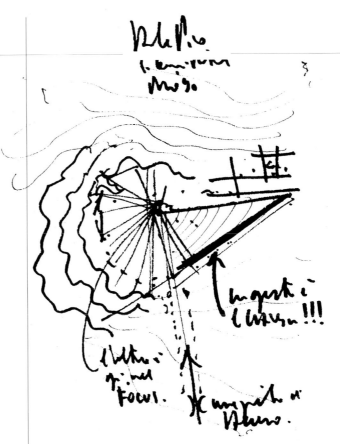

The plan is based around a snail's shell shape around which a series of huge stone arches support a shallow domed roof. The scale of the building means that the outer arches cannot span all the way to the centre so they begin to double up as the radius widens. Spanning up to 50m and comprising single stone sections of up to 2 tons in weight, these will be among the largest stone arches (if not the largest) anywhere. Piano uses stone throughout the structure as a unifying element; the structural arches, walls and fittings are all of stone. The stone floor finish continues to the parvis outside the building, drawing the external space within the confines of the building in an effort to include the entire crowd in the architecture and to minimise the distinction between inside and outside, a democratisation of the site. The complex curves and calculations needed for the stone structure and the cutting of its constituent elements were achieved using computer programmes which enabled the architects and engineers to utilise the full potential of the material and to

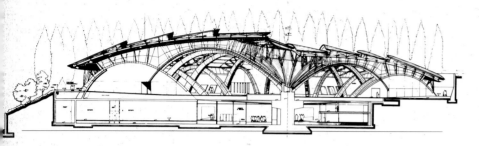

use stone in new ways, a kind of post-concrete reassessment of the oldest church building material. Piano's church seems to blend the organic, space-age spiral of Bruce Goff with the structural daring and elegance of his Italian forebear, Pier Luigi Nervi, whose magnificent stadia echo loudly through every aspect of this enormous project.

From an iconographic point of view Piano has attempted less than Meier in his Church for the year 2000 yet, despite this modesty (or lack of ambition), he has created a building with no less depth. Unlike Meier's sculptural interior which, with its bank of northlighting and great curving wall looks more like a sophisticated art gallery or concert hall, the interior of Piano's building genuinely envelops its core: the altar. Inevitably this will lead to a greater sense of community, of coming together, which embodies the key notion in liturgical reform since Vatican II. On the other hand, the sheer size of the interior has necessitated supports intruding on the central space and breaking up the unity of the interior which is essential to oneness. The temple, from primitive through Classical and Gothic ages, is often seen as an embodiment of the clearing in the woods, the archetypal space of worship and sacrifice. With arches and supports flying about throughout the interior and breaking up this space the notion of columns defining the edge is lost, the space becomes more forest than clearing and consequently less clear. It could be argued that Richard Rogers's circus

tent at Greenwich would make a finer, more focused centre for mass worship with its clearer definition and rational distribution of pylons.

Piano's church combines a kind of technical virtuosity, which could well conflict with the desire to create a simple, elegant space within which worship is the focus, with a simplicity which looks both naive and elegant. Surrounded by trees and approached beside a long wall housing bells, the huge shallow dome will become apparent as a revelation, very much as would the clearing in the woods. The terracing designed to house the outdoor congregation recalls the Greek theatre set into the landscape, the hills and the architecture working in one great dramatic, pantheistic gesture. The nature of the shallow dome too will inevitably bring comparisons with pagan archetypes, the sacred burial mound and the image of the cosmic mountain. There is something appropriate in these primitive analogies – this, after all, is a shrine to a holy man. Padre Pio's stigmata recall the image of the shaman, the holy man and the wounded healer (part witch doctor – curing ills, part mystic and priest), an archetypal figure who can see beyond this realm, in visions, in flights to the heavens. The shamans of Central Asia conducted their mystic rites within a yurt, the circular tent of the nomadic Mongols which is still in use today. At the top of the tent a central oculus allowed the smoke from the ritual fire to escape through the roof. The soul of the shaman, transubstantiated as smoke, was thought to fly to the heavens through this hole, it is the architectural expression of the third eye. If we look at the drawings of Piano's church we can see that the plan revolves around a hub: a single hole at the centre of the tent-like dome which allows light to penetrate the space below. This is a cult building as much as a church.
Edwin Heathcote

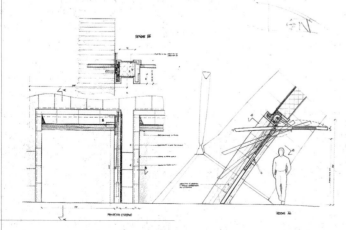

COSMIC ARCHITECTURE   **FOR 5,000 YEARS**

CHARLES JENCKS
MILLENNIUM UNVEILS POST-CHRISTIANITY

The unlikely truth of Britain's Millennium is that it is founded on a series of accidents; the fact they were subsequently polished up to look inevitable does not make them any less a matter of luck. Indeed, accident presented as design characterises the national celebration and supports my point: the Millennium Experience, to use one of its official titles, shows that Britain has entered a new era – Post-Christianity – even if somewhat absent-mindedly. That is probably the best way to enter a new era.

The first, although least important, accident is the timing. Assume for argument that the moment of Christ's birth was not fortuitous, that God did intervene in human history, it is still true that the precise date of divine providence is impossibly vague. It varies by three or four years, depending on scholarly opinion, the vagaries of the Christian calendar and whether one should celebrate 1999, 2000 or 2001. As Stephen Jay Gould has shown, the answer to this conundrum depends on cultural background.[1] The intellectuals favour the usual Christian convention and for example, 1601, 1701, 1801, 1901 and the populace favours round figures: the triple zero. This being the century of polls, and politicians who have to stay in power, the outcome was predetermined. In spite of the popular film *2001: a Space Odyssey*, there was no debate. The countdown for 2000 started in the 18th century and any country, such as Switzerland, which waited an extra year faced the double spectre of being new old-hat, yesterday's futurism – and nothing is more out of fashion than last year's new. In the rag trade it is called 'dead stock'.

Yet, Christ's birthday is the lesser of the contingencies. Except for the Vatican, a quasi-nation, no country has given deep thought to what the Millennium means. When, in Britain, the idea of celebration started to crystallise in the late 1980s it was seen as a moment to mark time. A great party and some public works

were imagined, but no Big Idea emerged. Then, in the early 1990s, John Major launched the ever-popular notion of a Lottery, and this led to the second great accident. It produced more cash than a North Sea Bubble and, in 1995, receipts of £5 billion per year. This success, eagerly welcomed, turned out to be embarrassing for it dwarfed the imagination – what is worth this amount? The result was the obvious compromise. Instead of one project for the nation as a whole, five 'good causes' were created, with an ambiguous public/private dividing line. No one could tell what was taxpayer's money, semi-public money, Treasury money, your money. To further confuse the issue of whether the year 2000 celebrations and the Lottery were the same institution, the five good causes were given five separate agencies, more than one of which could give out money to the same cause. The money could come from The National Lottery Charities Board, The Heritage Lottery Fund, The Sports and Arts Councils of England, Scotland, Wales and Northern Ireland, The Arts Council and, of course, the Millennium Commission itself. Those with the quickest business plan were most likely to get double funding.

The idea seemed good at the time. Filthy lucre, gambling money would trickle from the top down, while a myriad of pure, democratically induced ideas would percolate from the bottom up. Like many British compromises this had some virtue, especially in decentralising power and involving different parts of the country. But it also led to endless equivocation, and the funding of many questionable schemes.

Inescapable Question
Yet an even greater problem was the existential one, caused by the *embarras de richesses* which dropped from the sky. The

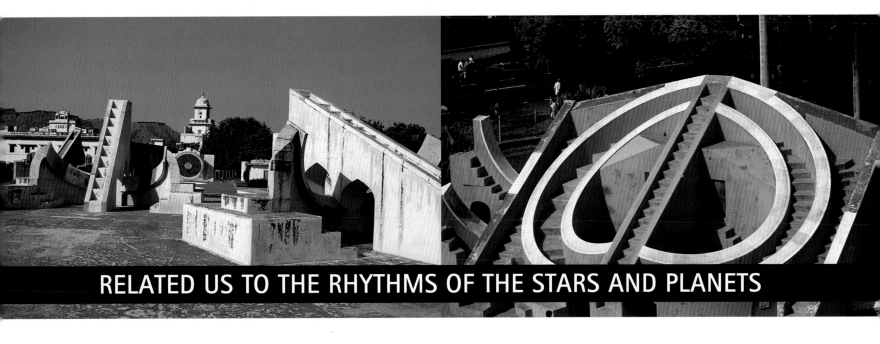

windfall forced Britain to confront a question it did not want to ask: 'Who are we?' With so much discretionary cash to spend the question became inescapable. One cannot tuck away £25 billion, that is $40 billion, into the pocket. True, most of this went to individuals who could suffer their accidental fortune in private, but the pressing question was collective. If, as said, Britain gained an empire in a fit of absent-mindedness, then at the throw of the dice it gained an identity crisis.

Thus it was not long before it discovered a silver lining to the question, albeit a third accident of history. As is well known to anthropologists, there are over 3000 tribes which still affirm their identity by carrying around a 'centre-of-the earth pole', a marker which they can stick anywhere and which instantly confers on the spot centrality and peripherality, us and them, the establishment and outcasts. The great thing about the round earth is that it provides an infinity of centres, all equally valid. One day Good Chief New Lab Blair, following the example of tribal leaders in New Zealand and other points where the sun is thought to come up first, discovered this truth and announced to the world – 'We are at the centre.' Yes, the answer to the British identity crisis emerged out of a hat. He had discovered Greenwich Mean Time (pretty mean on other cultures that want to be first). His words, as he launched the justification for the Dome, on 24 February 1998 – 'WHY THE DOME IS GOOD FOR BRITAIN' – put the following argument: 'Greenwich is the place the Millennium begins. If it was Paris Mean Time, don't you think the French would put on a show? If it was Berlin Mean Time don't you think the Germans would do likewise? When I was last in the United States people were already talking about how Britain would be the focus of the world's attention in the year 2000.'[2] Eat your heart out, rest of the world, your clocks strike to Greenwich Mean Time, our time – 'We are the centre of time.' And so, quite logically, the Millennium Commissioners located the centre-of-the-earth pole, the Dome, not in Birmingham where it might have been, but exactly where the longitudinal marker pointed: east London.

Still, even with clever discovery and relocation, the first accident would not go away. Christ's birth had to be faced and this became, as the countdown progressed, more and more the big problem for the country. Put it this way: most of Britain is partly Christian, celebrating birthdays, weddings, funerals and Christmas with Christian ceremonies and symbols, and those very same people may have an imperfect notion of what Christianity is, who Christ was, or in what it is necessary to believe. These truths have been pointed out since the 1960s, since the 'honest to God' debate, and a book of that name. For instance, although some 60 per cent of Britons say they believe in the Christian God, less than 12 per cent are regular church-goers, and perhaps only half that number are theologically aware Christians. The remaining 40 per cent are from other faiths, such as Islam, which are growing in both numbers and devotion. An unwelcome conclusion lay ticking in the year 2000 time-bomb. In terms of religious practice and conviction, Britain is one of the last Western countries which deserves to celebrate Christ's birth – unless a Lottery windfall is a sign of divine grace.

This fact explains what would otherwise be a perplexing event. When Tony Blair, a devout Christian, came to launch the Dome, he made no mention at all of possible Christian content! His speech was full of high-flown rhetoric and ideals of every kind. It described the value of 'tapping in to the creative talents' using 'the finest artists, authors, architects, musicians, designers, animators, software makers, scientists ... the Best of Britain' (authors and artists were, later, to hurl back these claims, in anger). It described bringing 'the nation together in common purpose' and a 'Millennium Experience' which would be etched in the mind of every child in Britain; and it said this experience would be part 'Disney World, Science Museum and West End Musical – yet different'[3]. In short, it promised a late 20th century mass festival, but nothing to do with Christ.

Scandal

Inevitably, this oversight dismayed the established Church and those 10 per cent who still cared. In several editorials the *Daily Telegraph*, unofficial guardian of this opinion, pointed out the lacuna and the void in British life it implied. A survey which it conducted with Gallup pronounced the shocking headline story: only one person in six links Christ to the Millennium.[4] The outcome of this poll was such a surprise that Gallup asked a revised question, but got virtually the same result. When report-

THE SUN, MOON, 24 HOUR CYCLE – OUR BODY & BIRDS

ers then asked Church leaders why the public was so confused, they 'blamed the Dome ... for compounding the evident confusion about the real significance of the Millennium'. However, once people were reminded of the real significance, one-third of them thought like proper Christians: instead of the centrepiece of the Dome being an hermaphroditic man/woman, they wished it would be a figure of Christ. (Actually, the hermaphrodite was preferred, even before it was seen, by 42 per cent).

Polls are notoriously vague and misleading because they do not usually catch the depth and intensity of people's beliefs. But they do tell us something worth knowing, especially in an age that uses them to determine the direction of political and economic life. Low results marginalise and high ones legitimise an issue, and the public issue at stake with the Lottery windfall became ever more pressing with each tranche of £5 billion. They implicitly posed the question: 'What do the British believe, today?'

What Gallup explicitly found out was that most Britons, by a margin of three to one, thought the Dome was 'a waste of public money'. (One should point out: it was not the architecture, but the contents they condemned.) The fact that the Prime Minister denied there was a penny of public money being spent, and the fact that the Millennium Commission was set up not to fund what the public wanted – which was spending on the National Health Service – was overlooked in the questions behind this survey. Yet, even if the pollsters were playing by different rules, how did the British want their billions spent? It turned out that 59 per cent wanted better hospitals, 25 per cent better schools and universities, 5 per cent a new national sports stadium, 4 per cent some exhibition different from that inside the Dome, 3 per cent 'other', and 2 per cent local street parties. As the *Daily Telegraph* commented: 'The responses could scarcely have been more negative.'

However, two things should be said. First, it is the government that should pay for these social functions as part of its normal duties, especially because the Lottery was explicitly designed for something else. Second, a moderate percentage, 21 per cent of those polled, admitted that they would visit the Dome whatever the contents, which would produce an acceptable payback of £200 million. Yet it is pointless to raise such logical points, when

so much money is around; floating cash always becomes subject to people's desire, and then politics. What no one could predict was the question it posed.

With an official price tag of £758 million, the Dome had become the unavoidable symbol of the identity crisis I have mentioned. Large impersonal forces put things on a collision course: 2000 years of Christian history hit a British culture that might be called lapsed-Christian. A multi-billion jackpot hit a 'dome', actually a tent with 12 pylons sticking out of it, like the crowning thorns of a crucified Christ. Unintended symbolism? With such political and economic weight riding on the year 2000, it became hard to take a neutral position. Even those who wanted to celebrate 'time', or the modernist notion of progress, were drawn into the debate. Arbiters of taste, such as the design and restaurant entrepreneur Sir Terence Conran, were quoted saying religion was not the fundamental issue of 2000. More radically, the youth culture impresario James Palumbo, a close friend of the then millennial conductor Peter Mandelson, 'said that all traces of religion should be removed from the Dome as young people found the subject boring and irrelevant. [Palumbo's] Club, the Ministry of Sound, revealed that it had submitted plans to turn the Spirit Zone into an all-day, all-dancing rave venue.'[5]

Such leaks, and counterleaks, fanned the culture war already fuelled by the cash. Not only was it a question of the image of Christ versus a man/woman hybrid – that is, religion versus humanism – but youth culture versus high culture and, as if these antagonisms were not enough, creative content versus corporate branding. Disney branding, logo competition, trade-fair warfare threatened to overwhelm Shakespeare & Co. Those corporations funding the 14 sectors were what Blair and the government firm, the New Millennium Experience Company, called euphemistically, '21st century companies with social responsibility'. Social responsibility? Such defence contractors as GEC, many nationally-styled firms – British Telecom, British Airports Authority, British Airways, British Aerospace – then large conglomerates such as Manpower, Tesco, Boots and the McDonald's chain. In effect, these ultra-socially-conscious and highly righteous multinationals were putting up £150 million in exchange for certain advertising and franchise rights. For instance, McDonald's

gave £12 million to become an official sponsor and build a feature called Our Town Story, an arena where 250 towns and cities tell the history of their area. A liberal politician claimed this sell-off to fast-food chains, chemists and defence contractors, , meant the Dome's celebration was degenerating into 'something of a trade fair'.

In launching the Dome in February 1998, Tony Blair had claimed the Best of Britain would be at the heart of the enterprise: the most daring and bold, 'the finest artists and authors'. By the end of the year two leading artists, Damien Hirst and Rachel Whiteread, were about to pull out because the place of art had been reduced to a token; and leading authors, AS Byatt and Michael Holroyd, as well as publishers and even the British Council, voiced 'disbelief that literature and language seem not to qualify [for the Dome] ... not even the Bible.'[6] Somehow Chaucer, Shakespeare and every other great writer were not the Best of Britain. What was so deemed? A time capsule featuring the Spice Girls, Tamagotchi computer pets, a pair of dirty trainers and such products as baby-pig feeders, shoes that do not need polishing and a waterbed for cows. Cows got a bed, Chaucer got the axe. Before he was driven from office, the trade and industry secretary, Peter Mandelson, who oversaw these choices, justified them as signifying the spirit of the age and for turning successful businessmen into 'heroes, on a par with pop stars and footballers.'[7]

A familiar pattern has emerged. Like the Olympics, the Year 2000 celebration is not only a trade fair but also a trade-off of values, a battle between the rhetoric of 'common purpose' and the reality of getting Mammon to pay for it. As his price, Mammon extracts his pound of culture. As with the Olympics, the architects fare rather better than the artists, the animators than the theologians. In an age of mass spectacle and Late Capitalism, the balance falls on the side of the quick and generic, especially in the Dome where 30,000 people per day have to see things at a continuous 2 mph. Something had to give, and that was religion, and art.

Those representing the Church, especially Stephen Lynas, Canterbury's officer for the Millennium, put a brave face on what they would be allowed by the situation, the fun and games

imperative. Just maybe there could be a short 'Millennium moment' – not too obtrusive, hardly noticeable really – when perhaps the 'gift of a candle' could be presented, along with, say, a Millennium resolution for New Year's Eve 2000 – call it the 'new start' concept. This was it. Daring, visionary, the Big Idea? Two thousand years of Christianity culminate with candles and 30 seconds of prayer! It was just possible, this breakthrough, as long as the BBC and other impresarios didn't determine it would turn off the hard drinking and raving. Focus groups would find that out. But then the secular imperatives started to bite. The Spirit Zone, failing to get its £5 million, cut back Eva Jiricna's steel and glass crystal structure and turned it into a £3 million tent. Ignominy? There was more to come. This transformation of steel into cloth was initially backed not by Christians but rather the Hinduja brothers, who dipped into their £1.2 billion fortune. Favourites of Baroness Thatcher and John Major, these beneficent Hindu entrepreneurs became the white knights of the Spirit Zone – Oh! *Esprit Nouveau*, Oh! Brave New World – until, finally, a Christian financier took up some of the slack.

It is wholly appropriate to look on this fiasco, and all the rest, as a good opportunity for apocalyptic prediction. After all, why else have a Year 2000, a celebration of the past and the future, a comment on what has happened and a foretelling of what will come? Many fortunes have been made out of this mark in time, much hype has been spilt and foolishness said. So, in the spirit of millennial cataclysm and *The Book of Last Things,* let me point out the lesson for the future and predict how the next 1000 years will turn out. What the Millennium shows is now clear.

Post-Christianity – Some Definitions

Many surveys in the West, over the last 20 years, have shown the decline in organised religion and a slackening in doctrinal belief. By contrast, there has also been a slight increase in a generalised spirituality with more people saying they believe in a vaguely defined divinity. The fall in church-going is not quite balanced by the rise in new nature-oriented religions and cults, but obviously some trade-off is occurring. At any rate, classical Christian religion has become very much a minority worldview. According to a 1990 Gallup survey in Britain, the previous 10

THE FINALITY OF DEATH   TODAY THE STREET   EVEN SHOPPING!

years had seen a loss of faith in such things as heaven, life after death and the presence of God in everyday life. While 70 per cent then said they believed in God, many added that they thought He does not influence the way they behave, nor have any great consequence in politics or real life. What kind of religion is this?

It is weak, selective belief and it is most apparent when it comes to wishful thinking. While 53 per cent believe in heaven, only 25 per cent accept hell; while 64 per cent think there is reincarnation, only 30 per cent say that Satan exists. Such upbeat optimism characterises a secularising society that tries, in the words of a Monty Python ditty, to 'always look on the bright side of life'.

Americans, of course, are even greater believers in a sunny God who has overcome the dark forces of evil. In a 1989 *Newsweek* poll, 94 per cent of those interviewed said they believed in God and 77 per cent said they believed in heaven; three-quarters of those said they thought they stood a good chance of getting there.[8] What surprised analysts of this was the discovery that God's victory was complete – hell had disappeared. As Walter Truett Anderson put it:

Nobody other than a small minority of fundamentalists believed in [hell's] existence, and nobody even appeared to be much interested in the subject. 'Hell disappeared,' a church historian said. 'And no one noticed.' It had been quietly fading away for a long time apparently – along with Calvinism and other visions of a stern and punitive God – and research revealed no mention of it at all in the indices of several scholarly journals of theology. Even the Roman Catholic Church, although still officially committed to a belief in the possibility of eternal damnation, had virtually nothing to say about Hell in documents such as the publication of Vatican Council II.[9]

By 1992, when its teachings were updated, the Church had secretly dropped all mention of limbo, a fact that was not noticed until 1999. By leaving limbo out of the revised catechism the Vatican hoped to forestall criticism that it was exclusivist. The danger was that unbaptised children would end up in no-soul-land, between heaven and hell. The Church was caught in an unfortunate contradiction: its doctrines had insisted that only baptised children could get to paradise, while popular opinion believes strongly in the innocence of unbaptised children and their

right to heaven, especially if they have died accidentally. Also, it seemed that all well-behaved humans should have equal rights to God's side. Since the modern and Post-Modern worlds have extended the abstract notion of rights to animals and ecosystems, it seemed churlish of the Church to deny to virtuous non-Christians the right to paradise. But since previous doctrine insisted otherwise, the only way out of the contradiction was silence, and a belief that time would sort it out in the end. Limbo, like hell, will go, and all that will remain are good things and paradise.

The same selective optimism is everywhere today; even cosmologists and ecologists adopt a similar mind-set. Very few want to face up to the dark side of the cosmos: its destruction, waste, kitsch, ugliness, bad design, pollution by killer asteroids – all the things which used to be called evil. Yet, even if this attitude is escapist it shows the cunning of reason, as Hegel called it, some progressive qualities, and these lead to the first definition of the new belief-system.

1. Post-Christianity is selective à la carte Christianity. No doubt a complete consensus has never existed among the faithful, but today nominal Christians, following habits of choice natural to a scientific community and consumer society, take what they want and leave what they dislike. On one level, this is religious shopping; on a more profound level, it represents deeply held beliefs combined with rational choice. When most American or Brazilian Catholics practise birth control, or reject part of an encyclical which is meant to be binding, they do so in the same spirit as they make other choices. Rational decision theory, weighing the pros and cons in a calculus of means and ends, is too ingrained to be relaxed when it comes to the big questions.

The First Vatican Council of 1869 may have declared the pope infallible when he speaks *ex cathedra* on eternal truths, but 93 per cent of American Catholics, when polled by *Time* magazine 100 years later, thought he was still fallible. Counter to doctrine they believed 'it is possible to disagree with the Pope and still be a good Catholic'.[10] The notion of infallibility was forged to counter modernism, Darwinism and the unchristian discoveries that were coming from science. It was the attempt to become a religious King Canute and hold the tide of

knowledge back. In some places it was politically successful, with the result that Catholics in these countries were systematically uneducated and kept from speaking freely. Hence the recent reaction, the mass conversions in South America to evangelical Protestantism. Ironically, in setting up the thought police, the Church has alienated thinking Catholics, many of whom regard the pope with dismay.

The attempt to be absolutist in the Post-Modern age has had the result of creating further dissent and breakaway groups – formal ones such as Catholics for a Free Choice and informal ones called 'Second Culture Catholics'.[11] If one is used to shopping every day and making the complex choices that an advanced industrial state demands, one is not going to change habits because of a proclamation. And so the total commitment which the Church demands, and used to get (at least in appearance), becomes impossible, except for a few.

When, because of the Church of England's decision to ordain women priests, many Anglicans decided to become Catholics, the leader of the British Catholic Church, Cardinal Basil Hume, tried, in 1993, to close the door with a slam of doctrinal purity: 'There is no question of becoming Catholics by accepting our teaching à la carte. You have to eat the menu or go to another restaurant.'[12]

It is interesting that, in discussing doctrinal matters, the cardinal himself adopts a consumerist metaphor, for it may lead to unintended inferences. In a restaurant, one eats freely; therefore, in church, Catholics should worship freely? An age of scepticism and the hard sell, Millennium hype, makes one suspicious of all institutions in their entirety. Even the pope himself makes selective liaisons with other religions, indeed anti-Catholic institutions, where they share similar doctrines. On a rational level this freedom, and maturity of choice, is a real gain. It leads to the second proposition.

2. Post-Christianity is the affirmation and criticism of its predecessor.
This double action, for and against, is shared by other movements such as post-Fordism, post-Darwinism and post-Socialism. Postmodernism, briefly defined, means 'the continuation of modernism and its transcendence'; that is, it accepts the liberating aspects of modernity, its democracy, concern for human rights, and creativity, while rejecting, or resisting, the attendant ecological and social destruction. In this sense, Post-Christianity is, simply, critical Christianity, but the doublethink also contains a complex form of denial. In everyday practice, in church, it means becoming deaf to pieties while accepting the aesthetic qualities that have been worked out over 2000 years, the beauties of ritual, music and spirituality.

The Spirit Zone of the Dome generalises, as a cultural anthropologist might do, some universal rites of passage, transitions that are marked by various religions. These are presented as generic, abstract, common to everyone at all times. But, with Post-Christianity, it has become normal to customise these universal transitions, to design one's own marriage ceremony and sometimes, even, one's own funeral. The way contemporary medicine allows one to extend life and die at home has meant that this rite of passage has become much more volitional, subject to personal design. Yet these Post-Modern ceremonies of marriage and dying are usually adaptations of Christian practice and, in any case, many non-believers still use the Church to observe moments of passage.

3. Post-Christianity means the end of the modernist settlement.
When the Church fought the Copernican worldview, when it fought Galileo and other modern scientists, when the Hundred Years War proved that doctrinal disputes would be lethal, an implicit settlement was forged. Science was given one part of the world, Caesar's part: truth, knowledge and the investigation of nature. Religion took the other part: morality, the soul, sentiment and pastoral care. This Modern settlement, effectively a Cold War with non-aggression pacts on a series of issues, almost broke down in 1859 with the publication of Darwin's *The Origin of Species*. Atheism nearly became a party political force and the public stance of scientists and academics. But, in spite of a few minor battles, the settlement held and each side stuck to its territory, clearly marking the boundaries. The Vatican drew ever clearer lines in the sand, creating 'infallibility' and that agency of political correctness: the Congregation of the Doctrine of the Faith (today run by Cardinal Ratzinger).

COSMIC ARCHITECTURE CONTINUES TO CELEBRATE

NATURE AND CITIES GROW AS FRACTALS

However, in the 1990s the Vatican moved towards science and reversed its previous teachings on Galileo and Darwin. Natural selection was allowed to be more than just 'a theory'. The Bishop of Oxford followed suit and declared that evolution is compatible with God's work. Thus theology tried to reconcile itself with contemporary thought.

This noble endeavour, showing how impossible it is to keep lines in the sand today, also created a great problem for God. For, if He is good, then it is hard for Him to use the unsavoury methods of Darwinian evolution; that is, competition, survival of the fittest and mass killing. There is no denying that Darwinian evolution depends on decimation, the killing of nine in ten, in order for the tenth to pass on its genes. One way out of this moral quagmire is the post-Darwinian position: that nature works with more forces than the nasty ones. Another escape, which Post-Christian believers use, is to argue that God is not all-powerful, that He too works with nature and does not control it. This is an acceptable, if woolly, trade-off: if it robs Him of traditional omniscience and omnipotence, at least it restores an ethical sensitivity – and what is God if not good?

The Post-Modern age is characterised by shifting boundaries, fuzzy categories and overlapping disciplines. It's impossible to keep religion and science in their modern pigeonholes. Even 70 years ago, changes in science and spirituality had started to erode the settlement. Developments in quantum physics showed that in determining the objectivity of results, science had to take into account the instruments and focus of the observer. They also showed nature was indeterminate, fuzzy and as much like a lightweight subtle idea as a heavy hard particle. Along with the general theory of relativity, it showed the universe really was a unity – radically so – just as religions had always claimed. Everything is interconnected across a warped space–time, which itself expands as a unity. These, and many more discoveries of science, had implications that turned out to be quasi-spiritual, implicating knowledge with the knower and the known.

By the 1970s chaos theory, complexity theory and ecology showed, in other ways, that the universe is a dynamic, self-organising whole. Again the implications are somewhat spiritual, or at least animistic, because we can now understand ourselves as being directly related to the unfolding and highly creative cosmos. According to the modern worldview, as Newton characterised it, matter was massy, dead, hard and impenetrable. The planets moved like clockwork, the universe was a machine. In the last few years, as nature and the universe were discovered to be self-organising and dynamic – not predictable and mechanical – the outlook changed. In effect, because of such discoveries, the modernist settlement smudged out and the boundaries between science and religion had to be redrawn.

This change is evident in the many books written by scientists, recently, with God in the title. Some of them are spoofs, some are opportunistic ways of selling books and some are based on a misunderstanding of what is traditionally meant by God; but some, like Paul Davies's *The Mind of God*, redefine both sides of the science/religion border dispute. In his book, Davies quotes the astronomer Sir Fred Hoyle: 'The universe looks like a put-up job, as though somebody had been monkeying with the laws of physics.'[14] Is this the sentiment of a scientist or a metaphysician? Fred Hoyle rejects the Big Bang for the Steady State and other models of the origin of the universe, and he spends his time asking the fundamental questions and doing basic research, with a ferocious tenacity. He observes: 'I have always thought it curious that, while most scientists claim to eschew religion, it actually dominates their thoughts more than it does the clergy.'[15] In so far as this is true, it leads to the next point: that Post-Christianity is led partly by scientists.

4. Post-Christianity develops from Christian rationality, monotheism and the belief in an abstract law-giver. Why did it not develop where it seems most at home, from Hinduism, Buddhism, Taoism or the more pluralist and nature-loving traditions? These have been influences on the emergent consensus because they see all things as animated and in the process of becoming; yet they did not accentuate the notion of a rational, discoverable nature. Western science developed out of the Christian belief in a rational God whose laws were clear, consistent and not whimsical: as Einstein put it, 'God is subtle but not malicious.'

For the year 2000, in all countries, science has played a larger

RAW STONES FROM EARTH

WAVES AND TWISTS IN LAKES AND MOUNDS – GRAVITY WARPS SPACETIME

role than traditional religion in celebrations – at least in terms of *les grands projets*, as the French called their landmark schemes in the 1980s. The science museum with a difference, as Tony Blair phrased it, has become the model for such things as Liverpool's National Discovery Park, Leicester's National Space Science Centre, Glasgow's Science Centre, The Deep (aquarium) in Hull, all costing well over £30 million, the benchmark for landmark status. From comparative figures of funding, one might well imagine that a scientific view of nature has replaced both an aesthetic and religious perspective but, as the content and design of these projects reveal, that is not quite the case. It is spectacle and science translated into sound-bites that is triumphant, science with a difference, indeed.

Whatever the failings of the millennial view of the universe by Disney, it is still true that the unified programme of science has only developed from the Western assumption that all of nature's laws are consonant and unified. Monotheism, as opposed to Hindu animism and pluralism, leads to the Western pursuit of the Holy Grail: that is, the search for the grand unified theory of the universe, not the many ad hoc hypotheses of a pluriverse. Or, it leads to the theory of everything, as it is called with hubris. Such a theory may some day unify the fundamental particles and forces – hardly everything, but it does stem directly from the Christian attempt to understand God's abstract laws. Only if you believe, passionately, that God designed a rational, ordered world will you seek to decode it. In this sense Post-Christianity could have only developed in the West after the period of Christian rationality, this leads to a counterproposition.

5. Post-Christianity also means non-Western Christianity, the importance of non-Western religion and ecological spirituality. Just as the Post-Modern world describes the globe after the Asian economies have challenged the West, after world communications have decentred Western power, so Post-Christianity entails a religion that comes after we know the importance of non-Western religions. As Charlene Spretnak has argued, it is the rediscovery of the central role that the great wisdom traditions are playing in deepening moral thought.[16] Buddhism, Native American spirituality, the goddess cultures and the Abrahamic tradition (which includes Judeo-Christian and Islam) counter the mechanistic worldview with a relational one.

This is shared with the ecological paradigm, the motive idea behind so many of the Millennium projects, both in Germany and the UK. If there is a single Post-Christian ideology it oscillates around a fuzzy centre circumscribed by the Greens, the ecological movement, nature worship and the Gaia theory. There are tensions between the groups that make up this loose movement, but it is coherent and strong enough to have dominated most of the large landmark projects. A partial list of the large schemes reveals the consensus: there is Doncaster's Earth Centre and Edinburgh's Dynamic Earth; Cornwall's Eden Project and Newcastle's Centre for Life; Liverpool's Pondlife Centre and Gloucestershire's Wetlands Conservation Centre; Merseyside's Wildflower Centre and Kew's £80 million Millennium Seed Bank. Above all, there is the UK-wide, 2785 miles of Millennium Cycle Route – given a grant of £43.5 million (quite a lot of bicycle path).

When it comes to religious expression itself the obvious emphasis is on the ecumenical spirit, both for good reasons and bad. Since spirituality is a mode of experience common to religions, just as aesthetic experience is common to art, many people today are willing to mix practices and hybridise beliefs. They do not approach spirituality with the attitude of a lawyer, of a theologian disputing points of scripture. The result of this tolerant hybridisation can be messy and opportunistic, or idealistic and creative. In overseeing the Spirit Zone, Stephen Lynas pulled together Anglicans, Baptists, Evangelicals, Methodists, Roman Catholics and others, not worrying about doctrinal differences. As I mentioned, the Hinduja brothers, who helped fund the Spirit Zone, accepted the primary place of Christianity, but they explicitly asked for a recognition of other faiths: of the Muslims, Jews, Bahais, Sikhs, Jains, Zoroastrians and Buddhists. The Spirit Zone had the onerous task of representing such plurality without offending anyone, of being spiritual in general. Except for the cross, specific symbols and imagery that would alienate other faiths were placed in the background. Eva Jiricna managed to design a generalised, expressive subject that was unusual, striking and therefore open to new, spiritual interpretation.

6. Post-Christianity is shot through with Christian assumptions which it cannot ditch. This and the next proposition can be looked at negatively because they are both unavoidable. This forces the ironic question: Can the West be anything but Post-Christian? The European languages reflect the notion of the soul, personal responsibility, guilt for breaking one's word and the idea of right thinking. These are deep metaphors that motivate action. A child in school is taught to question different sides of an issue and make a choice that will weigh on his or her conscience. He is also taught respect for the individual, and that life (human if not animal) is sacred. Of course, Asian cultures have similar values but somewhat less emphasis on the individual. They do not accentuate and dramatise individual choice. A Japanese or Chinese Hamlet, while conceivable, is rare.

The West produces individuals who wrestle with their souls every day, and celebrates them in the lives of the saints. Artists live out the same struggle in public, and a central part of Western literature of introspection and doubt is based on the private conscience. From St Augustine to Dostoevsky is a straight line. Even the daily newspaper thrives on the minutiae of contradictory psychological states. When Prince Charles, barring his soul in public, exposes his angst-ridden doubts to the close-focus of a TV camera, the audience immediately recognises the type. Here, if not quite Greek tragedy, is psychodrama on a royal scale. A Japanese prince would never play the tortured Hamlet, could not think and feel like this and, certainly, the Japanese government would not allow it.

While most people have given up the Christian idea of an immortal soul, they still keep a very strong notion of its first cousin: the responsible self. How else to explain the fanatical outbreaks of political correctness, or the fact that today Deconstructionists make such a point of cleaning up what you think. To have the wrong thought in the West means you feel guilty, or that you must be made to feel remorse until you purge it; in the East it is shame not guilt that is most important. Political correctness may exist in both East and West, but only the latter has turned it into an heroic (and much-lampooned) category.

7. Post-Christianity is failed or lapsed Christianity. No one will argue with this unfortunate truth. We are in a Post-Christian epoch because Christians have stopped believing in their foundation myth, ideologies, set of rules and eschatology. Non-practising, non-believing Christians, those who attend church at Christmas, weddings and funerals, are Christians in name only and by far the largest group. They observe the conventions because rituals are spiritually moving, or aesthetically satisfying; or because they wish the Christian message were true; or because, socially, they have to go to church; or because there is not much else on offer; or because, like Clinton, they have to get elected to office. Most politicians are post-Christians: they do not get the votes unless they mouth the pieties and break the Christian vows (they often have to tell lies, favour the strong and rich, and do other things Christ condemned).

If Christ appeared today, it is said, he would not be a Christian. Gandhi expressed a similar point with ironic precision. When asked what he thought of Western civilisation he answered: 'I think it would be a good idea.' So would the Christianity of Christ. But, since the early Church linked up with the remnants of the Roman Empire, the faith has become an organised, sometimes enforced, state ideology. It has favoured power and control more than Christ's principles.

This is not to say that many Christians are not motivated by his example and words, but rather that organised Christianity has adopted the 'things that are Caesar's'. It is an obvious point, left out of basic education: the Caesars, the Roman Empire, crucified Jesus and then, 300 years later, took over his name and message. This is rather like squaring the circle: people hope it works. The problem is it sows doubt. One reason people are post-Christians today is that Churches emphasise power and social observance: correct form and behaviour matter more than Christ's teachings. Thus some lapsed-Christians might be on their way to a more radical Post-Christianity such as liberation theology, but they have not yet reached this stage of consciousness. On the other hand, their loss of belief makes them ripe for new belief, and one of the contenders for this is the recently formed notion of cosmogenesis, the idea that the universe itself follows a process of self-organisation that is creative and in certain respects progressive and benign.

COSMIC ARCHITECTURE AS

8. Post-Christianity is an emergent faith in emergence. If the view from both cosmology and the Christian story is that the universe got us here through a series of stages, or jumps, then there is faith that in the future it may continue to help us through such leaps in organisation. This could be called animal faith, the basic instinct that, however cruel, the universe is a good place.

Christians, by contrast, emphasise the past, not the emergence of the new. The weight of the Bible, doctrine, history, architecture, power structures, habit – all these things – conspire to orient Christianity backwards. But now, thanks to complexity theory and a good bit of scientific research, we know how, and partly why, the new emerges suddenly from the old; we know that novelty is real, that the behaviour of whole systems emerges in an unexpected way and acts differently from the behaviour of the parts. The theory of emergence is quite different from the previous modern theories. Under Newtonian mechanics, and the deterministic world view, creativity was underplayed, or made a mystery. In the 18th and 19th centuries, the universe was understood to unfold in a linear, predictable manner developing along the model Darwin, among others, put forward. Post-Darwinists now realise this view, while not altogether wrong, is still not right enough. Species, individuals, even the universe as a whole, develop by jumps and by inherent, unfolding morphogenesis. Through constant feedback emergent systems become non-linear, and almost everything in nature is non-linear, slightly

changing, fractal in form: embryonic growth, the heartbeat, thoughts, landslides, the weather, galactic formation, supernovae. Only a few things, such as the orbit of one planet around the sun, are deterministic. Even two will, given enough time, send the system into emergent non-linearity.

If emergence is the general rule of an unfolding universe, then a Post-Christian metaphysics will start to reflect this. The implications are dangerous, liberating, creative and irreversible. We cannot go back to a deterministic, modern worldview, or a Christian one. We cannot not know the implications of complexity theory and many of the other Post-Modern sciences. That is why one can be optimistic about a change in culture. It is coming from science and beginning to be absorbed in every field of endeavour. It is only a matter of time, I believe, before Christianity takes the implications on board and catches up with the 'Post'. When it does so, let us hope that it tells the story of the universe better than it is being told in the millennial projects, the Earth Centres and Dynamic Earths. Cosmogenesis, the narrative of the universe as a single, creative, unfolding event, which includes us in the story, is our Genesis myth, a point of orientation and a story which gives the identity so lacking in the present to culture and individuals. The year 2000 events rightly started to focus on this unifying story but, sadly, turned it into a B-film. The universe, the Millennium, we, deserve more.

Notes

1 Stephen Jay Gould, *Questioning the Millennium*, Jonathan Cape, London, 1997.

2 Tony Blair, 'WHY THE DOME IS GOOD FOR BRITAIN', People's Palace, Royal Festival Hall, 24 February 1998; press release of speech, p2.

3 Ibid, pp3-4.

4 Philip Johnstone, *Daily Telegraph*, 14 March 1998, p1.

5 Nigel Reynolds, 'Dome served up with Girl Power and fries'. *Daily Telegraph*, 27 November 1998, p9.

6 Nicholas Heller, 'Hirst puts dome on ice', *Sunday Times*, 1 November 1998, p13. Dalya Alberge, 'Writers condemn the 'book-free' Dome', *The Times*, 2 November 1983, p1.

7 Martin Delgado, 'Dome to reveal Britain at its inventive best'. Evening Standard, 2 November1998, p3.

8 'God Slips in the Christmas Poll Ratings', *Sunday Times*, 23 December 1990.

9 Walter Truett Anderson, *Reality Isn't What it Used to Be*, Harper and Row, San Francisco, 1990, p202.

10 Ibid

11 Ibid, p205.

12 *Independent*, 24 April 1993, p1.

13 My idea of Post-Modernism as this form of double-coding has been extended by Linda Hutcheon in her *A Poetics of Postmodernism*, History, Theory, Fiction, Routledge, New York and London, 1988.

14 Fred Hoyle, quoted in Paul Davies, *The Mind of God, The Scientific Basis for a Rational World*, Simon and Schuster, New York, 1992, p199.

15 Ibid, p223.

16 Charlene Spretnak, *States of Grace, The Recovery of Meaning in the Postmodern Age*, Harper and Row, San Francisco, 1991.

DESIGNING IN THE DIGITAL AGE

Jane Pavitt

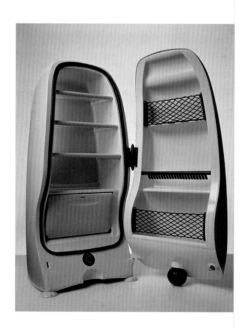

A recent ground-breaking exhibition at the V&A in London, 'Designing in the Digital Age' explored how design has responded to new technologies by looking at three everyday products in close-up: the Dyson DC05, the OZ refrigerator by Electrolux–Zanussi and BT's Synergy 1500 cordless telephone. Here its curator, Jane Pavitt, V&A Senior Research Fellow in Product Design, gives an overview of the history of CAD and takes a look at how it might be responsible for creating a new craft practice in product design and architecture.

The design of successful new products has always relied upon a combination of skills, ideas and technologies. Traditionally, we might have thought of the process of industrial design as one segmented into specialised stages. The client, the designer, the model makers and technicians, the engineers and the manufacturers all worked according to quite rigid distinctions, performing specific functions. The development of new technologies often challenged such distinctions; and provoked vigorous debate about the changing nature of skill and 'deskilling' as a consequence of mechanisation. During the 20th century, the design to manufacture process developed into a highly stratified linear process, where tasks and skills were managed separately, and often completed in isolation before the next stage began. The archetypal example was the Fordist production line, where increased mechanisation, standardisation and division of labour were the key organisational strategies.

Critics from Jean Baudrillard to Daniel Bell have described the characteristics of a post-industrial age.[1] The products of a post-industrial design culture, we are told, are more communicative and less standardised. Product design is now more concerned with the packaging of information and the mediation of the relationship between object and user. The 'digitisation' of society is generally seen as changing our ideas of both products and services.[2]

The advent of computer aided design heralds a greater role for design in determining our environment. Computer Aided Design (CAD) and its corollary, Computer Aided Manufacture (CAM), have prompted a re-ordering of the design process. As well as technical and organisational implications, this re-ordering is having noticeable creative and aesthetic effects.[3]

CAD was first developed in the 1950s for use in the aeronautical industry. In design terms, 3D CAD started to have a significant effect in the 1980s, when it was taken up by the automotive industry. The first stage in the assimilation of CAD systems into the work of product design and architectural studios was 2D CAD – a method of drafting on screen which replaced the lengthy and difficult process of producing technically and dimensionally accurate drawings for model makers and manufacturers. Once the technical data were rendered as 'soft' rather than hard copy,

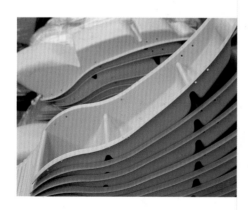

Oz refrigerator by Electrolux–Zanussi during manufacture and as completed product.

then adjustments could be made without the need for substantial redrafting. In the early 1960s, Chicago-based company SLS Environetics developed machines for drafting interior plans for architects, which replaced the more routine aspects of work in the drawing office.[4] With the development of 3D CAD and the possibilities of solid modelling and animation, computer aided processes are being utilised as creative as well as technical tools.

3D Computer Aided Design allowed for a radical rethinking of the design to manufacture process. 3D CAD allows the designer to model the product in three dimensions rendered as either a solid form or a 'wire frame' construction. Wireframe drawing is the forerunner of solid modelling, and is used as a means of viewing structure and assembly in products, or for creating perspectival and axonometric drawings.

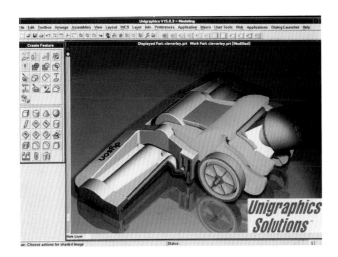

As the product or component is modelled, the software will calculate the physical dimensions of the form. As the designer introduces more product characteristics to the computer – such as scale, material weight, moving parts and so on, the 'virtual' product is created on screen. In the V&A exhibition, 'Designing in the Digital Age', we examined the creation of three products, showing how product designers work with a combination of design methods, creating both the virtual product and the physical model alongside one another.

Take one example: the designer wishes to create a product with a complex modelled surface, with curves and no straight lines. This is described to a skilled model maker, with the aid of sketches and some dimensions, and the model maker produces a foam or wooden scale model according to these instructions. This model is essentially an interpretation of the designer's drawings – and the sketches themselves are an interpretation of an idea. Once a form is agreed upon, the dimensions of the model must be plotted accurately so that they can be given to a manufacturer to produce tooling for a prototype. When Zanussi began their development of the 'Oz' refrigerator, their design studio had no 3D CAD facilities, and the first scale model had to be produced in this way, taking about three weeks in the workshop. Some of the more complex curved surfaces of the Oz could only be achieved later, once CAD had been introduced.

If the designer uses a 3D CAD-CAM system, then the modelling stage can be done on screen. By plotting a series of points and lines, the designer can construct an extremely complex modelled surface that would be difficult to render by more traditional techniques. The virtual product can be interrogated on screen – rotated through any angle, disassembled or have pressure applied to it to test its strength. The data can be exported to machines capable of producing accurate prototypes. A range of processes known collectively as 'rapid prototyping' is used to create actual size components or moulds from resin. Rapid prototyping uses lasers to cut forms from solid blocks, or build them from fine skeins of liquid resin (rather like icing a cake). They can be ready within a matter of hours. Rapid prototyping is rather like 'printing out' an object in three dimensions: one of these processes is called stereo-lithography.

The widespread use of rapid prototyping suggests that the traditional craft of model making is now obsolete. In reality, design studios tend to use a combination of the two methods – making card and foam models early in the process and using rapid prototyping later on. At Dyson Appliances, for example, the two methods of model making are combined as the designers develop the product simultaneously in virtual and physical form.

There is a close relationship between the creation of the screen-based model and the handmade model. The Hoxton-based model makers Gavin Lindsay & Co moved into the production of digital visualisations a few years ago, when they realised that digital models were more often

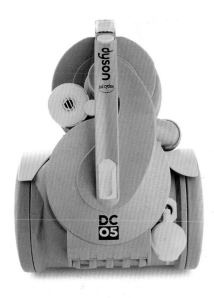

Cutaway computer image of the latest Dyson Dual Cyclone vacuum cleaner, which was designed in 3D with Unigraphics Solutions CAD/CAM software, and the completed product.

BT Synergy 1500 cordless telephone as shown created in Unigraphics Solutions revolutionary 3D Computer Aided Design (CAD) software, and the completed product.

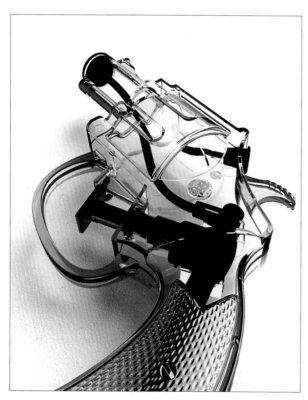

Computer-generated image of a water pistol by Solid State Industries Ltd.

being used for advertising campaigns and other presentational work. They now do a variety of work with both handmade and rapid-prototyped models, but most of their work is in digital format. The company produces digital models for photographic work and presentations, and has worked with designers such as Ron Arad and Jasper Morrison. Using the CAD package *Alias*, they create virtual models with realistic surfaces, finishes and even 'built-in' imperfections. Skilled in the art of model making, they bring an understanding of craft skills to their use of CAD.

For many independent design studios (as opposed to in-house design departments) rapid prototyping is done off site. Although some are now investing in having such technology on site, the assimilation of it into standard studio practice is slow. But this is only a matter of time – as Ron Arad points out: 'We used to go to the corner shop to use the photocopier until we decided to buy our own.'

The decline of model making is only one aspect of the transformed design process. 3D CAD also allows for a closer relationship between designer and manufacturer, as they are more likely to be working from the same 'soft' data. As long as software systems are compatible, the procedure for translating a designer's drawings into technical drawings for tooling manufacture is much simpler. In principle at least this means that the integrity of a designer's work is less susceptible to alteration, and the concept less likely to be 'lost in translation'. With the increasing likelihood that the designer and manufacturer may be located in different parts of the globe, the compatibility of CAD systems is even more necessary. One typical example is the BT Synergy phone range – designed in Britain by alloy ltd, but engineered and manufactured in southern China. The designers and manufacturers were able to maintain a dialogue despite the distance, by dealing with one set of compatible product data. As in other areas of life and work, information technology compresses both time and space, speeding up processes and overcoming geographical distance.

CAD is also a highly effective presentational tool, a vital factor when presenting concept products to clients. Reading technical drawings takes skill and familiarity with the codes and conventions of such images. All areas of design, particularly architecture, benefit from the ability to present the client with a 3D CAD rendering of a product or a fly-through of a building environment. There are drawbacks to this – a product that appears 'finished' when it is still at the concept stage may not prepare the client for the inevitability of future changes. Nevertheless, the use of CAD helps clients to think of products as real rather than abstract, even when they are in early concept stages.

A New Craft Practice?

There are parallels between the use of CAD and the idea of craft practice. The separation of the design process from the process of fabrication is a characteristic of 20th century industrial design, but not craft production. As design writer Tom Mitchell once put it:

> The idea of 'The Product' as an object considered in isolation from its context of use did not exist before the advent of industrialisation, nor did design professionals who planned, but did not construct products. Before industrialisation objects were made using craft processes in which the planning and making of objects were inseparable aspects of the same processes.[5]

The inseparability of planning and making is also a characteristic of Computer Aided Design. Malcolm McCullough and Peter Dormer, among others, have argued that the use of digital technology is itself a form of craft practice, where the hand–mind split engendered by industrialisation is restored.[6] Designers should be able to embrace the possibilities of CAD, not only as a more effective substitute for the existing stages of design development, but as an alternative form of creative thinking.

Ron Arad began to integrate the use of 3D CAD into his studio about six years ago. As a generation of computer literate designers emerged from college, bringing new skills with them, the studio recognised the need to keep pace with what Arad terms 'the digital revolution'. The studio realised that the complexity of CAD was a means to achieving imagined products and structures. Major projects such as the Tel Aviv Opera House were being developed using traditional design methods – the opera house was presented to the client as an 'artist's impression' – but these methods were time-consuming. The introduction of CAD helped the studio to render projects by more efficient means.

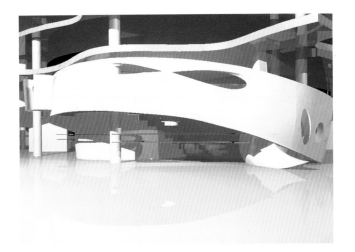

Isolated computer image of island in main foyer of the Tel Aviv Opera by Ron Arad and Alison Brooks.

One of the dangers of CAD, however, is that it makes the means of achieving a 'finished' concept far too easy. The seductive quality of CAD images can disguise inadequacies in the work. 'Give anyone a synthesiser,' says Arad, 'and it doesn't make them into a musician.' The rapid spread of CAD goes some way to account for the glut of organic forms in product design and packaging at present, a dominant aesthetic made more possible by the tools in the hands of designers. The challenge of CAD is that it is more than just a timesaving and efficient styling tool, and can offer designers the chance to conceptualise products in different ways.

Ron Arad's most recent work explores the relationship between the real and the virtual product, using rapid prototyping as an end in itself, rather than as a developmental stage. The 'Wire Frame Vase', shown in Milan in the summer of 1999, an object made by rapid prototyping, gives physical form to what is meant to exist only virtually. By giving physical properties to the lines of the wireframe image, the screen image is able to be made in actual three dimensions. Arad also embedded text into the virtual image, so that this too would be 'printed out'. The text reads, 'This is a unique piece. The computer file used to generate this object was destroyed on 15th March London 1999.' Rapid prototyping is a process that can be repeated endlessly, without the 'original' data deteriorating. Arad has inverted this idea by destroying the data, rendering the object unique.

Arad's latest project is the 'Bouncing Vase', the 'original' of which is an animated computer file. The vase – designed as a coil or spring – jumps across (and out of) the screen. The movement is 'captured' in a series of frames, rather like an Edward Muybridge series of photographs. By selecting a frame and sending the data to be prototyped or 'printed off', a physical object is created. The object can exist in several hundred variations, each a different configuration of the same data. The 'Bouncing Vase' shows how CAD can be exploited to produce new kinds of objects, wherein the hierarchy of process and object is reversed. In this case, the process is the object, and the physical product that results from it is actually just a by-product.

Arad's work is just one example of how CAD can be used to re-conceptualise the design process and create new kinds of objects and forms. So far, the impact of CAD-CAM can be seen in terms of timesaving and design-to-manufacture accuracy, but its greatest impact may well be upon the creative process of design.

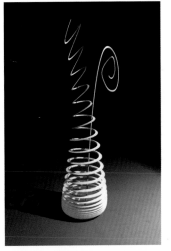
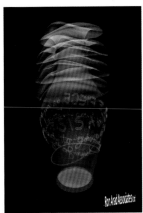
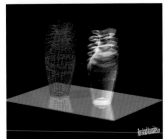

Ron Arad Associates, Vase Images, August 1999.

Notes

1 Jean Baudrillard's essay 'System of Objects', in John Thackera (ed), *Design After Modernism: Beyond the Object*, Thames & Hudson, 1988; Daniel Bell, *The Coming of Post-Industrial Society: A Venture in Social Forecasting*, Basic Books, 1973.

2 See Nicholas Negroponte, *Being Digital*, Hodder & Stoughton, 1995.

3 Most noticeably, research into product aesthetics and computer-related design is taking place at the RCA, under the tutelage of Anthony Dunne & Fiona Raby. See Anthony Dunne, *Hertzian Tales, Electronic Products, Aesthetic Experience & Critical Design*, RCA, 1999.

4 Giuliano Zampi & Conway Lloyd Morgan, *Virtual Architecture*, Batsford, 1995.

5 Tom Mitchell, in Thackera, op cite, p209.

6 Malcolm McCullough, *Abstracting Craft; The Practised Digital Hand*, and Peter Dormer (ed), *The Culture of Craft*, Manchester University Press, 1997.

When art meets architecture

Parisian Housing by Frédéric Borel

Robert Such

Frédéric Borel works and lives in Paris. He qualified in 1982 after studying at the Ecole Spéciale d'Architecture. He started his career under Christian de Portzamparc before setting up his own practice in 1985. To date, his projects are those mentioned in the text, plus the Valmy-Recollets crèche in the 10th arrondissement. His main preoccupations are the interplay of space, form and a sense of movement; providing sensorial (both physical and visual) pleasure; creating an opening between the street and the more private domain of the courtyard. Borel also concerns himself with the ethnic background and social needs of future tenants in a culturally diverse metropolis. In so doing, he injects the 'imaginary' into his work and produces low-cost rather than low-quality housing.

'They are not ready for me yet,' concedes French architect Frédéric Borel whose recent block of flats at 131, rue Pelleport, 15, rue des Pavillons (1998) in the 20th arrondissement has become a Parisian east-end eye-catcher. They being the city's authorities, the manager behind the Left Bank urban development zone, ZAC Rive Gauche, in the 13th arrondissement.

Undergoing a slow process of accretion around the much maligned Bibliothèque Nationale François Mitterrand, the ZAC, with its eventual 5000 apartments, will comprise one-third low-cost housing, or HLM. So far Borel's efforts to get a foot in the door have proven unsuccessful.

Limited risk-taking on this major redevelopment site, which has become a pawn in the 2001 municipal elections, facadism – bulldozing everything but the facade – in traditionally bourgeois quarters, and private developers' conservatism means there is little scope for anything too radical. Yet with significant long-term regeneration of run-down areas in eastern Paris, the HLM market enables young architects to cut their teeth, yielding some surprising returns.

The 40-year old Borel shares the inclination of his mentor – Pritzker-prizewinner Christian de Portzamparc – for bold, emotive colours, lyrical and rhythmical shape-making within a three-dimensional framework. He involves the eye, permitting it to weave across volumes and space, tying up the pieces, sorting out ambiguity.

At rue Pelleport, Borel has reworked his preferred language into an exuberant exhibition piece, while at the same time incorporating a 'technology' room for teleworking.

At the base a large orange foot, or brake, seemingly prevents the whole mass from slipping away down the road, and rather than nestling into the surrounding framework, the block of colourful, slim and sleek walls and columns jostle for room.

Nevertheless, his very expressive style, pattern-making, and collages of various com-

Frédéric Borel, 131 rue Pelleport, Paris, 1998.

ponents – of Classical inspiration, sculptured objects, Minimalist 'artworks', futuristic monoliths that double as housing blocks, or vice versa – could be disconcerting for purists.

This does not concern Borel: 'I'm not a purist; I'm for complexity,' he says, adding that 'I'm interested in the contrast between the city and the microcosm, [and in particular at 113, rue Oberkampf (1994), 11th arrondissement] between the more archetypal forms using a very simple vocabulary while placing the more futuristic towers in front.' Such that the horseshoe colonnade to the rear of the rue Oberkampf site symbolises background historical 'depth' with the tall, tapering columns in the foreground.

Contextual considerations came first, however, as Borel explains: 'Around [rue Oberkampf] there are a lot of heterogeneous buildings: some very high, some very low. The first thing was to create the empty space, because there are no gardens in this quarter. Then we put together the two complementary architectural objects – one turned towards the sky, the other towards the earth – to find an original dimension with respect to sky and ground with architecture.'

At roof level, apparently guarding the 90m deep by 20m wide central area filled with bamboo are 'The Three Heads', which bring to mind the silent, stone deities on Easter Island. This figurative analogy can be extended to 100, boulevard de Belleville (1989) in the 20th arrondissement, where three imposing sentinel-like buildings demarcate the border between street and courtyard.

Although now a fashionable 1990s signature mark, the sinusoidal roof, which caps one of the giant sentries, conjures up a more fluid version of Oscar Niemeyer's Church of St Francis at Pampulha (1943) outside Belo Horizonte with its free double-curving form. (Searching for the Brazilian connection in Borel's work points towards Portzamparc, who cites Niemeyer as an inspiration for the Cité de la Musique.)

Borel exploits, yet again, a long, narrow plot by organising ground-floor commercial space and residential quarters around a heart in which local residents congregate and children play.

'I always try to find the private space for the building,' says Borel, 'and at the same time an opening onto the city – to increase the symbiosis.' A theme that he followed at 30, rue Ramponeau (1989) with an open staircase and look-out balcony over the

**Frédéric Borel,
113 rue Oberkampf, Paris, 1994.**

**Frédéric Borel,
100 boulevard de Belleville, 1989.**

narrow street.

Theoretically, 'the sounds from the street can sometimes be nice,' but, according to residents at boulevard de Belleville, an echo-chamber effect causes noise to resonate within the walled enclosure. Thus, an unwelcome invasion of the interior occurs rather than a pleasing one. Curved walls also make life's practicalities and simple tasks difficult – where do we place the bed or how do we arrange the furniture?

Through its ups and downs low-rent accommodation has made steady progress over the past century. Rethinking the way forward takes us further from the brick ghettos of the HBM (office of public housing, from 1914 to 1937) and the 1960s and 1970s low- and high-rise monstrosities.

An important sea change came about in 1975 with Christian de Portzamparc's Les Hautes Formes, Impasse des Hautes Formes in the 13th arrondissement, which gave individual features to each apartment around a square and passage, while present-day public bodies involved in building and refitting, such as OPAC, RIVP and SGIM, are reforming their architectural policies and choosing who to carry them out accordingly.

Veteran urban designer Antoine Grumbach, a favourite of OPAC, considers that 'a city is not a collection of architectural objects. It is the shape, the form in itself, in which public spaces are more important than buildings.'

Situated along one of the narrow, quiet roads in the old village of Ménilmontant in the 20th arrondissement lies Grumbach and Didier Gallard's 44–6, rue des Cascades (1998). Punctuated by metal balconies and other small surprises, notably the rhythm of fenestration, the collection of flats, duplexes and artists' workshops display overtones of Northern European style, Scandinavian chalets with pine shuttering.

A far cry from Borel's 'integrated' art, Grumbach here tackles the layering of the city, resulting in the contemporary and restored standing comfortably together, indicating two strands of thought on the Parisian scene.

'In terms of respecting the memory of the place,' proposes Grumbach, 'the city is never an achieved object; it is always characterised by permanent inachievement. You cannot start a project without knowing the process, the different transformations that have happened in an area. It could be from when it was a field to when it became little houses, then buildings, then the history of industry. So, by under-

standing the mechanism of formation of the place you can find the way to create a building or public space which seems in coherence with the place, and not to create objects totally disconnected from the environment.'

Yet how can 'sewing up' the urban fabric in a banal or brutal context create sustainable architecture?

In Borel's 1997 notes 'Density, Networks, Events' he takes the view that 'We must implement a careful mix (of colours, shapes and materials) and inject "imaginary" into the new emotional wastelands that contemporary cities are tending to become ...' and in Borel's book that takes architecture into the realm of art.

Frédéric Borel,
30 rue Ramponeau, Paris, 1989.

Christian de Portzamparc,
Les Hautes Formes, Paris, 1975.

Grumbach and Didier Gallard,
44-6 rue des Cascades, Paris, 1998.

The City of Psychogeography

Iain Borden

Iain Sinclair's numerous psychogeographic writings have explored cities as places of strange corners, unknown symbolism and odd encounters. Yet these writings have their own secret history, being derived from revolutionary Situationist ideas of the 1950s and 60s.

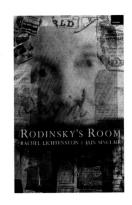

If you take a close look at urban culture today, it can sometimes seem as if every artist with a sense of the street, every graphic designer with an eye for the everyday, every advertiser attuned to the benefits of guerrilla-graffiti promotion, has caught on to something new about the city: it does not have to be rational, clean, ordered and nice, but can be wholly irrational, dirty, disordered and even downright nasty. Busshelters become transformed into temporary works of art, clothes are reconfigured by jumble-sale jewellery and street-market finds, and everyone from Sony to *Blueprint* is sticking bill posters on to lampposts and phone boxes. This is the city of psychogeography, where one gives oneself (and others) over to the accidental and hidden facets of urban life, revelling in its possibilities for play and rebellion, odd objects and strange events. Even the Sunday paper literati are part of the spell, with novelists and prose-producers pumping out the weird words faster than the Thames spews out into the North Sea.

Foremost in this psychogeographic lit-pack is Iain Sinclair, whose numerous outpourings on the secret history of London have most recently included *Liquid City* (Reaktion, 1999) a collaboration with photographer Marc Atkins, and *Rodinsky's Room* (Granta, 1999), another collaboration, this time with artist-turned-writer Rachel Lichtenstein. Sinclair's books are intensely personal excursions into the city, detailing the forgotten worlds of the City, Brick Lane, Greenwich, Silvertown and the like (Sinclair is particularly keen on London to the east of Farringdon Road) as if they had only recently been uncovered after years beneath the mud flats of the river. His inventions, mixing lyrical description and idiosyncratic obsession with acute observation and precise historical recall, evoke the

city as a dark dreamworld into which the past bubbles up and in which the future, if it is visible at all, is but a tiny ray of light at the end of the urban forest. Above all, Sinclair's prose suggests that the city belongs to everyone, that anyone can head off into these atmospheric corners of the city, armed only with an old map, a battered notebook, a 35mm Pentax, and a desire to go where no *Guardian* reader has ever gone before. Go head, they exhort, reinvent the city according to one's own whims and idiosyncratic walking, make up new routes and hookup unlikely connections, observe odd architectural details and note down blue plaques, while entirely resisting the lure of the pay-to-enter museums, McDonald's and mass-market malls that make up the rest of the city. Make an anti-consumerist statement: ponder, don't purchase.

As this suggests, however, something else lies hidden beneath such private afternoons, something far more politicised than the refusal of a Big Mac or the V&A's pricing policy, than the wandering through the backstreets of the East End. Back in the 1950s and 1960s, the psychogeographic ramble through city streets was but one tactic in a welter of such actions promoted by French film-maker Guy Debord and the rest of the 'Situationist International', an enormously influential group who, far more than just a collection of individual artists and creative producers, aimed at nothing less than the complete transformation of life into a revolutionary condition of experiment, anarchy and play.

Disturbed at what they saw as the ever-heightening infiltration of state capitalism and socialism into the everyday lives of their citizens, using the spectacle of the image in particular to alienate people from their creative potential (the 'Society of the

Spectacle'), the Situationists instead proposed a series of tactics to resist the modern state, to resurrect the individual and to redefine creative life. If the major targets were pretty obvious – capitalism and Stalinist socialism – the way to enact this critique was not. Whereas political protest in the past had focused on the ballot box or the coup, the organised demonstration or the full-on revolt, the Situationists wanted to invoke a real and complete revolution through that most pervasive of sites and times: everyday existence. Not for them the big, coordinated protest, not for them the inauguration of a new political party; what the Situationists wanted was to change life itself, and to change it now. As you would imagine, the later events of 1968 were hugely influenced by Debord and Co.

To enact this revolution of the everyday, the Situationists stressed the kinds of place and tactic that everyone had access to: the street, one's own body and thoughts, play and sex, random behaviour – small yet ultimately highly important things that the state could not (or at least had not yet) managed to control and routinise. Their tactics were both highly idiosyncratic and precise. Central to them was the notion of *détournement*, by which existing elements of city life – ideas, objects, space, buildings, codes, imagery – can be appropriated and re-used. Hence the famous 'Naked City' diagram by Debord shows a street map of Paris cut up and re-pasted, (ie *'détourned'*), with particular centres of 'psychological intensity' joined together only by a series of red, fat, twisting arrows. This is Paris as a military campaign, a series of targets and sites recomposed by sorties out into the urban field.

Unlike military rationality, however, the driving logic of the psychogeographic city is, as its name suggests, the very emo-

Constant, New Babylon Nord, 1958

Constant, New Babylon

Guy Debord, The Naked City, 1957

Constant in his studio

tions and passions that any good general would want to suppress in his troops. Not for psychogeography the precision of the parade-ground drill; rather it involves such things as the *dérive*, which is a kind of alert, constructive and transgressive 'drift' across city spaces. A *dérive* often means connecting places together by purely accidental means, such as setting off to walk across Paris while armed with a map of Berlin, or by a psychogeography, where decisions about where to walk next are made not by reference to an authoritative architectural guide or tourist map, but by some form of individual, subjective response to the emotional contours of the urban landscape.

In this way the rational, planned city becomes something else. In place of maps, one has journeys; in place of certainty, one has to rely only on uncertainty and aleatory encounters; monuments are replaced by everyday architectures such as road signs and brick walls; objects are recast as events, with different meanings at different times. The whole of the city becomes knowable less as a set of squares, placenames and fixed boundaries and more as a set of ambiguous atmospheric qualities – what the Situationists called 'unitary urbanism'.

From these kinds of action, on which the research and writing methods of Sinclair are often directly based, it would be all too easy to conclude that the Situationists focused entirely on the everyday urban experience of things which already existed. However, apart from experiencing things, the Situationists also wanted to make them. And the way to do this, they conjectured, was that just as routine acts like walking should become more critical and experimental – something more creative and artistic in the widest sense of these terms – so should the reverse happen, and all innovative art practices should become more 'everyday' in nature. Although they themselves, under the leadership of Debord, soon let go of art and pushed toward ever more theoretical and placeless utopias entirely devoid of any creative practices, their ideas on art have had enormous influence ever since, ranging from avant-garde movements like Fluxus

to more popular phenomena such as the punk subculture of the late 1970s and the road protest movements of the 1990s. To give but one example, Patrick Keiller's films *London* (1993) and *Robinson in Space* (1997) are both highly indebted to Situationist ideas and tactics, being based around seemingly erratic journeys across London and the rest of the UK, while recovering vital facts and observations ranging from the residences of Daniel Defoe to the annual freight tonnage processed through the country's container ports.

But it is in architecture that the Situationists may yet have their greatest triumph, some 40 years after their initial urban explorations.

The problem facing the SI was, then, how to construct such spaces. One possibility was the *détournement* of old city forms, but the other, as followed by Constant Nieuwenhuys, the Dutch SI architect, was to propose new architectural forms. The resultant 'New Babylon' projects were consequently a series of complex, contradictory spaces and designs, using the language of Constructivist architecture and sculpture to create spaces of Baroque technological complexity, dynamic labyrinths in which flexible partitions, atmospheric conditioning systems, ambient coloured lights, lenses used as windows, movable staircases, echo rooms, deaf rooms and other such technologies were disposed within a massive megastructure floating 16m above the existing city. In such a construction, Constant tried to follow fellow-Situationist Asger Jorn's assertion that 'we do not recognise the existence of architecture,' and to design not objects but force-field 'quarters' of the city that created atmospheres such as the Bizarre, Happy, Useful, Sinister, Noble and Tragic, or Historical.

Unsurprisingly perhaps, New Babylon has never been built, and exists only as a set of drawings, models, texts and paintings. Instead, the Situationist architectural designs and ideas have been most successful when appropriated and 'popularised' in the 1960s and 1970s by the French Utopie or Italian Superstudio groups, or, in the context of some rather different libertarian politics, by the British Archigram.

And in the 1980s and 1990s, it has been this architectural route which has most consistently re-promoted Situationist ideas back into the city. Whether in the hands of architect-theorists like Bernard Tschumi and Nigel Coates, who expound architecture as a place of event and situation as much as of form or fixed place, or through numerous smaller, less well-known but equally switched-on practices dotted around the cities of Europe.

Situationist-inspired architectural ideas are creating architecture of an extraordinary range and inventiveness: temporary structures from rave marquees to rock concert stages, culture spaces from zooed-out bars to innumerable unknown shops, residences from squatter appropriations to high-spec loft fit-outs. These architectures share a notion that everything can be grist to the mill, from industrial metal to retro-chic chair design, from ripped-up magazines to highly sophisticated printing techniques; these are spaces that encompass early morning quietude as well as late-night debauchery, reflective thinking as well as high-octane bodies. They are architectures in which to be active, to do things, to produce.

Above all, these are projects which each, in their own small way, suggest that the Situationist city was never meant to be a purely private affair. Yes, by all means re-invent the psychogeographic city in your own head by walking along its streets, but never for one minute should you dare to think that this city is consequently exclusively your own, yours to possess as a private dream-city. Too often, those contemporary drifters one spies in Bethnal Green or the Royal Docks, drunk on one too many Sinclair texts, seem to be engaged on little more than romantic tourism: one more photograph for the collection, one more sketch before bed-time. Against this, a really gritty Situationist urbanism means getting on with it in the company of others, in a city where other people meet and converse, agree and get annoyed with each other, and generally live and create. The situation, that's the thing, and a situation needs more than one of us to make it happen.

Brick Lane, London

Near Brick Lane

Royal Docks, London

Near Royal Docks

It's a long way from the city of Naples to the West Side of Manhattan. And it's almost as far, aesthetically, from the streets of 19th century row houses and quaint shops in Greenwich Village to the raw concrete meat lockers and rusty warehouses of the meat district a few blocks north. But Ada Tolla and Giuseppe Lignano, partners in LOT/EK who moved to New York to study architecture at Columbia University in 1990, live right on the edge in every sense – on the meat-packing side.

When Tolla and Lignano, who met at the University of Naples, moved their studio to a small industrial building in 1992, the meat district was just that. Scents wafted through the cobblestone streets from carcasses hanging in wholesale butchers' storerooms. Trucks, lined up perpendicular to the street, unloaded freshly slaughtered beasts or filled up with packaged foods for delivery elsewhere. Upstairs rooms in the industrial buildings on both sides of the wide, angled streets seemed abandoned, but so did a dilapidated, brick, flat-iron-shaped hotel, though it thrived, in its way, as a gay flophouse. Then a photographer moved into a big bare space. Another rented a loft nearby. Industria Studios built spaces for photo shoots in the neighbourhood. Models and actresses flocked to Hogs'n Heifers, a rough hillbilly bar where patrons dance on tables and fling their bras on the bar. The old, block-long Nabisco cracker factory was converted to a gourmet food market with an outlandish flower shop, fresh fish, fancy bakeries and party rooms.

Now, half a dozen art galleries, two Belgian restaurants and a boutique have arrived. By night limousines ferry leather-clad, multipierced young hipsters to edgy clubs. But by day, the carcasses still hang behind steel doors, and trucks outnumber taxicabs and pedestrians, ten to one. And on the north end of the meat district, tawdry warehouses and garages have been converted to create the West Chelsea art gallery district. Here Soho pioneers have moved to avoid the clothing stores and busloads of gawking tourists attracted by their own success in creating a gallery district further south.

American Diner No 1, Tokyo, Japan.

Giuseppe Lignano and Ada Tolla of LOT/EK at the Chicago Art Fair.

LOT/EK

Here Jayne Merkel architectural writer and editor of *Oculus*, takes a trip to the edge with young New York practice LOT/EK. Merkel shows how the urban debris of a meat-packing district of the city has provided them with the inspiration for a gritty and highly individual vision of fun-filled architecture.

Guzman Penthouse, Midtown, New York, 1996.

LOT/EK still toils away on small, low-budget or temporary projects, even as its celebrity grows. The architects work out of a small, third-floor, walk-up loft where Lignano lives behind a tractor trailer wall on castors. They feed on truck bodies, bring them inside, turn them into rooms, furnishings and restaurants.

The American Diner No. 1 which they designed for a client in Japan was to have been made of two bright red shipping containers set side to side with a gap in between so sunlight could penetrate both spaces. The restaurant name ran in big white letters around the entire volume like a logo on a truck body, only bigger. One volume contained the dining room; the other housed the kitchen and bathrooms. The design was supposed to be a prototype for a restaurant chain, prefabricated and fitted with interiors in the US and shipped to each location abroad. But it was never built.

Neither was the Goree Memorial, a competition scheme for a museum of the slave trade and navigation in Dakar, Senegal. Red containers with smaller white lettering and cut-outs for windows were to hold exhibits and serve as symbols of the vessels that brought slaves across oceans as cargo. Other truck bodies – or parts of them – have turned up in the Miller-Jones

Studio/Residence and the Guzman Penthouse in Manhattan. In the Miller-Jones loft, a 40-foot-long aluminium shipping container divides work space from the living quarters. When the panels are closed, all you can see are TV screens, but they can open to unveil a kitchen bit by bit, and link the two spaces. An old refrigerator body set on its side serves as a workstation, with a drafting table mounted to one end and a computer terminal to the other.

The Guzman Residence, in the shadow of the Empire State Building, has a penthouse made out of a bright yellow trailer planted on the roof. A section of roof had to be cut away, so that one end is a kind of deck (framed by the trailer edge with red reflectors), because the whole container would have created a larger addition than the zoning allows. (The building was almost built to the maximum volume zoning allows before the architects began converting an old mechanical room into an apartment.) Walls and shelving in the rooms below the penthouse are also built with container walls and other detritus of the urban wilderness. A fire escape connects the living room to the shipping-container bedroom on the roof.

At a recent lecture in the Architectural League of New York's prestigious 'Emerging Architects' series (where almost every

Miller-Jones Studio, Midtown, New York, 1995.

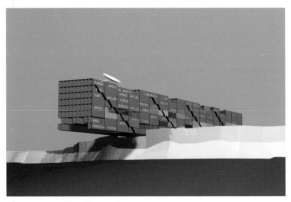

Goree Memorial, museum complex design competition, Dakar, Senegal, 1997.

famous architect in the city has made a debut), Tolla and Lignano illustrated how their ideas and materials came from the underside of the urban scene. Their perfectly orchestrated computer sequences flashed scanned-in snapshots of parking lots, overpasses, underpasses, alleys and super-highways on to a screen. In almost every shot, brightly coloured shipping containers with corrugated metal walls and big bold lettering appeared. Primary colours predominated, as did silvery metal skins. It soon became clear that where others see industrial waste, they see Pop Art and Lego-like cheap chic building materials.

An extremely consistent vision runs through the pair's very original observations of very ordinary things. They like basic geometric shapes: boxes and cylinders. They like strong colour contrasts: red, blue, yellow, black, white and silver. They like once-useful objects with a recognisable past, materials with a history and an iconography built in. LOT/EK's 'TV lamp' is made out of old TV screens, set within a pillar of cables and turned towards the floor and ceiling so that only the glowing light of the cathode ray appears, almost image free. Other light fixtures, the 'Chromo Lamps', used in their studio are made out of colourful and curvaceous empty detergent bottles. With their insulated wires showing, they resemble Christmas tree lights or strings of patio lighting, but they aren't even that pure. Their cast-off quality makes them seem sadder and sillier at the same time since their old identities linger.

Not only are their own light fixtures used in the industrial-strength LOT/EK Studio, glowing coloured light from neon tubes, television sets, and computer monitors reverberates. The work area also has an 'indoor billboard'. A three-part, three-dimensional, corrugated metal room-divider sets it off from Lignano's bedroom, where kitchen appliances present their backsides, all pipes and tubes and wires, for a Rube Goldberg effect. The bathroom, with silver walls and supergraphics, is at the end of the kitchen, overlooking an asphalt rooftop and the industrial edge of the Hudson River.

Tolla and Lignano turned the bright green cylinder of an oil tanker into a 'sleeping pod' at the Morton Loft, a long, high-ceilinged space in a former West Village parking garage. Another canister, set vertically, contains the bathroom.

With the same plucky aplomb, LOT/EK has designed a series of 'ballrooms' to accommodate benefits for the Brooklyn Academy of Music, a non-profit institution that for 25 years has been producing the most ambitious avant-garde musical programmes in New York. The first Next Wave Festival Opening Gala, in 1996, transformed a vast industrial space into an airport runway ready for a night landing. Hundreds of 18-inch-wide rental dining tables were set end to end in very long rows, creating a 1984 Orwellian refectory. The tables were lined in black plastic and lined up with a 12-inch gap between each pair, where 12-inch TV screens could be clamped face up to provide a modern kind of candlelight complete with ghostly images. Bright coloured tape defined each place setting and identified each table. Orange power cords hanging from the ceiling added vertical elements while they powered the light source.

In 1997, the architects used bare blue gelled fluorescent tubes running the length of the space to transform a warehouse in the Brooklyn Navy Yards into a dining room for 800 patrons. For this event, tables were set between gigantic concrete columns in rows across the width of the space, intersected by additional tubes of

TV-Lite modular television lighting system.

Next Wave Festival Opening Gala, 1996.

Video theatre for Chicago Art Fair, 1999.

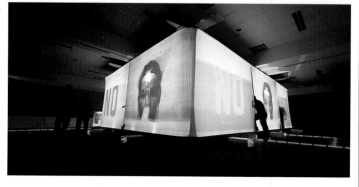

light lying across their tops in mirror images of the ones hanging from the ceiling. In order to saturate the space with ethereal blue light, object contours were neutralised by white tablecloths, white china and white chairs. LOT/EK created an illuminated intimate core within the gigantic industrial structure for last year's New Wave Festival Opening Gala with walls of milky tarp TK 230 feet long, 30 feet wide and 20 feet high and then projected predominantly red, moving coloured images of faces on to them. Three long rows of dining tables were set up inside these translucent walls; the entrance, coat check and dance floor were on the other sides.

They used similar glowing, image-filled, two-sided walls at the 1999 Chicago Art Fair on the Chicago Navy Pier, where core walls of white Spandex rested on an elevated, black, 24 foot by 30 foot platform under a ceiling of black Spandex. Red navigation lights directed visitors to the entrance core where four slits allowed them to enter; two other slits separated some film and video art programmes from others. Instead of walking around the room, viewers pivoted lazily in blue vinyl-coated lounge chairs which increased the fluidity of the 360-degree experience. Infrared remote headsets positioned on the seats relayed and controlled the sound of the programmes, which were rear-projected on to the core walls with large mirrors, effectively doubling their size while consuming only half the projection length of

the video projector. 'Ret.Inevitable 1.5' explored the physical aspect of total absorption in the cinematographic experience by saturating the viewer with a barrage of images intended to dematerialise the floor and ceiling. To do so, the architects forged a collaboration between FLMSCL (filmskool) and Electronic Arts Intermix (EAI).

The installation was one example of a way the architects are studying what they call 'the interaction of the human body with the products and by-products of industrial and technological culture'. Another was an exhibition at Deitch Projects, a gallery in Soho, in the winter of 1998, where a petroleum tank was sliced into segments like a salami, lined with foam tubing installed by the architects themselves, set sidebyside the way they were when the tanker was intact, and retrofitted with cable and remote control to activate the TV sets inside each module. Gallery-goers were invited to curl up inside and watch the programme of their choice. This writer found the copy editor of the magazine she edits curled up inside one on a Saturday night with a sandwich

TV-Tank

and proofs, working away. The installation, called 'TV-Tank', later travelled to the California College of Arts and Crafts. (The copy editor did not go along.)

For the vast and chilly landscape in between, the architects have proposed an even wilder cocoon – a 46-foot-high squished sphere to house the Chicago Indoor Skateboard Park. The bright green blob with round blue windows would sit in the landscape like a space ship on a landing pad. Bright red entrance tunnels would connect to the terrestrial universe. A 360-degree walkway around the middle would accommodate bystanders too weak or wise to scoop up and down the curved walls leading to the curved floor and ceilings.

The venturesome gyrations of the skaters seem an apt metaphor for the free-flowing creativity of these young bold designers who hang in there between the carcasses and sculptures, rubbing shoulders with truck-drivers outside their door, and the Greenwich Village poets a few blocks away, as they turn the useful grit of their city into lively, fun-filled art.

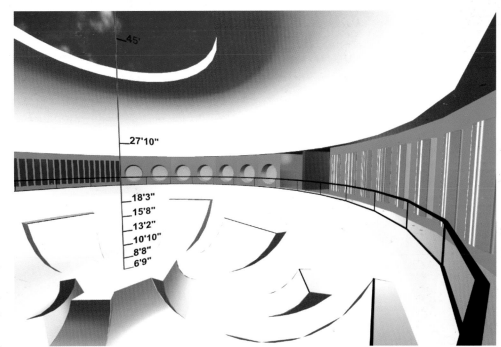

Interior and section of Chicago Indoor Skateboard Park.

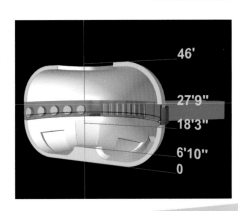

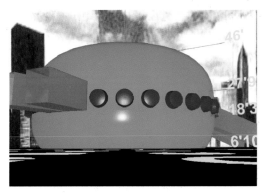

List of Built Works
(Date given is that of design)
Interiors:
1999 Klein Photography Studio, Meat District, New York
1999 M.A.O. Offices, Garment District, New York
1998-1999 Morton Duplex, West Village, New York
1997 Macmillan Penthouse, Soho, New York
1997 Tolla-Guidetti Apartment, Rome, Italy
1996 LOT/EK Studio 2, Meat District, New York
1995 Miller-Jones Studio/Residence, Midtown, New York
1995 Guzman Penthouse, Midtown, New York
1994 Produx, clothing store, West Village, New York
1993 Bernstein Apartment, Chelsea, New York
1992 LOT/EK Studio 1, Meat District, New York

Buildings:
1998 Indoor Skateboard Park, Chicago
1997 Goree Memorial, museum complex design competition, Dakar, Senegal

1996 Deitch Projects, art gallery, Soho, New York
1996 Guzman Penthouse Addition, Midtown, New York
1996 America Diner No 1, shippable restaurant for Tokyo, Japan
1994 Performance Pavilion, Lorraine Kessler Gallery, Poughkeepsie, New York

Installations:
1998 TV-Tank, television lounging tube
1998 Whitney Museum of American Art, proposal for the design of the American Century 11 Exhibition
1997 Surf-A-Bed, multiscreen channel surfing system
1996 DJ Tower, sets for music video of 'A Tribe Called Quest'
1995 CBS News, mobile viewing room for 'Eye To Eye', New York
1995 Museum At Fashion Institute of Technology, video theatre, New York

Events:
1999 Art 1999 Chicago, video theatre for Ret.Inevitable 1.5, Chicago
1998 Brooklyn Academy of Music, Next Wave Festival Gala, temporary environment

1997 Brooklyn Academy of Music, Next Wave Festival Gala, temporary environment
1996 Brooklyn Academy of Music, Next Wave Festival Gala, temporary environment

Products:
1998 Work-Wall, Home/Office wall unit for Ross/Bernstein's apartment
1998, Wire-Lite, dining light for David Leiber's apartment
1997 TV-Lite, modular television lighting system
1995 Wall/Thru, units for the home technologies
1995 Point & Shoot, Vitra Design Museum, Perfect Chair for Barbie in the 1990s competition, 2nd runner-up
1994 Chromo Lamps, detergent bottled lamp collection
1993 Electric Chairs, microchips of human/technological functions
1993 Bed/Room, convertible bedroom/living room
1993 Furniture Collection, workstation, stereo lounger, conversation double-seater

'With Perrault'

Vivian Constantinopoulos

Dominique Perrault Architect, Birkhäuser (Basel), Actar (Barcelona), 392pp, £49.00, HB, 230 colour & 350 b/w illustrations.

At first glance, the exact title of this book is unclear, since it appears to stretch from the back to the front cover – 30 names 'with' Dominique Perrault. If you pass your hand over the cover, however, the blocked letters would indicate that the title is 'With Perrault', while the title page reads 'Dominique Perrault Architect'. So, a standard monograph? Perrault's opening statement to the book tells us that this is precisely not a monograph; the book is intended to be a participatory exercise, a book in which 'visions, words, images intersect with diverse and multifarious readings of contemporary architecture...' He calls forth a 'shared pleasure' – one that has already been shared in the making of this book, which, while divided into buildings and projects, includes throughout responses from a variety of commentators – an impressive list of names from fellow architects to journalists and curators – on the works presented. As he says, the 'shared pleasure' is 'destined to be shared', thus presumably extending to the multifarious readers, who can then proffer their own interpretations.

Indeed the cover image itself implies sharing and participation: we can hardly see the building for the people – the users' movements in the space form the main element of the image, not the building (the Bibliothèque Nationale de France, shown later in the book). Yet this usage of space is not reflected in the imagery within the book, a large format publication of almost 400 pages.

Frédéric Migayrou's introductory essay elaborates this idea of participation when he tells us that Perrault's work is non-hierarchical; it is not about composition, but about forms, materials and the involvement of those in the project (one imagines he means by this that the development of the projects is organic in some way, feeding off the input of those participating in the creation of the project, rather than adhering to one idea from the master architect). Migayrou also terms the work a 'styleless' architecture; neither Modernist nor Postmodern, lacking a modern syntax. '... By neutralising architecture, Perrault invents a path leading to proximity in the architect's work, an architecture in act, a manifest architecture of the neutral.'

It is not surprising, then, to read that the jury for the Hôtel Industriel Jean-Baptiste Berlier competition nominated Perrault's proposed glass box as the winner. They, too, had an unclassifiable, neutral programme for a new type of building 'whose evolution could not be foreseen'. Which is what the building is – a shell enveloping an ever-changing space now housing various enterprises including a printing works, a homeopathic lab, photo agency, workshop for jobs for the disabled – as well as Perrault's own office.

Many of the photographs in this book include facades and facade details; not always enough in the way of drawings or more detailed views. Yet this seems fitting, since so much of the architecture – and discussion of the work – is focused on the facade. The commentaries on the respective projects are often about how the forms (whether styleless or not) position themselves on the ground. And, above all, how these works are encountered. The imagery is mostly blown-up; and, accordingly, the text is large type (although not as difficult to read as it first appears). In fact, the book seems rather overblown: it's big, but we don't always get much of an insight into the buildings. It is the kind of two-dimensional material that seems satisfactory for an exhibition (incidentally, the book was published on the occasion of a Perrault exhibition), but not for a book of almost 400 pages. Sometimes the large-size images are appropriate and look stunning (in particular the Berlin Velodrome); on other occasions, they are simply ill-fitting, such as in the presentation of an art installation project where two images are blown up over four large format pages, and the sense of the work is lost.

Nevertheless, the presentation works well with such projects as IRSID Centre, which is, in any case, a neat project. Here, an extension to a château that bears an uncanny resemblance to Hitchcock's Bates Motel, is set into the ground, beneath and around the existing building. This is a highly appropriate theatrical gesture. By extending the plan outwards and beyond that of the château, the château now sits on a glass 'plate' or pond, looking like a cake decoration. The extension 'base' is lit up at night, illuminating the château above (although it is a pity that we cannot see the night view in this book).

The obsession with surface doesn't work so well with the Bibliothèque Nationale's 'open books', however. Interestingly, Perrault invokes a complementary metaphor to the

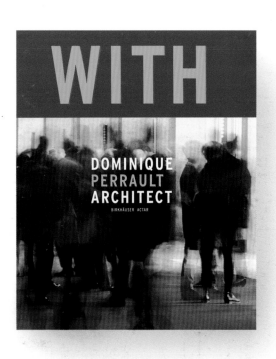

somewhat tired joke, calling the towers 'vertical labyrinths'. Yet a labyrinth is a place in which you can lose yourself, find your way, or accidentally keep reaching the same point. These towers are surely vertical axes, unmysteriously reaching for the sky, sheer forms with the design function of shelving books. Towers of Babel also come to mind ... Toyo Ito makes reference to Perrault's photomontage of the project concept: 'a monument to the dead'. Shouldn't a library be precisely the opposite – storing the books for access and *use*, gathering information to share with readers generation after generation? To counter this, Ito describes the building as more 'modest' in reality. This is true. The tower's monumentality does diminish on approach, as does our understanding of the facade, which looks warmer when we get a closer view of the wood slats. But does this temper the building's symbolism?

One wonders whether this isn't all to do with affect, or possibly effect: 'architecture produces emotion first of all, and this emotion is the keystone' Perrault states. But our emotional experience seems to be about our initial encounter with the building. As Migayrou points out, 'He confines himself to the founding event of an architectural "there is".' Yes, the buildings are undeniably 'there'; but, what next? Where is the use and the participation? However difficult it is to translate this into the two-dimensionality of a publication, it doesn't come through as powerfully as it could on the level of the imagery. The architecture seems to engage the viewer (the viewer, rather than the user) on a direct, but ultimately one-to-one level.

Vivian Constantinopoulos is Commissioning Editor at Phaidon Press.

'Cloning the Highlands'
John Richard

Miles Glendenning and David Page, *Clone City: Crisis and Renewal in Contemporary Scottish Architecture*, Polygon, 236pp, PB, £11.99.

Miles Glendenning, a historian and David Page, a practising architect, trace the evolution of the architect in modern Scottish society from late 18th and 19th century capitalism, through 20th century social democracy, to today's market liberalism, and argue that we have arrived at a situation of crisis and confusion. The culture of the global marketplace – postmodernity so the polemic runs – has led to a process of architec-

tural disorientation. What was once unique has become mere imagemaking, and relationships that were previously familiar and well understood are replaced by incoherent permutations. On the one hand, there is the architecture of the isolated self-referential 'signature' buildings turning their backs on the real world, and on the other hand the banalities of standard housetypes in residential suburbs. The cloning of 'Dolly' the sheep is the hook on which the authors hang the argument that 'clone city' is a threat to architectural and personal identity.

If this was all that the book had to offer it would be no more than a squeak of protest from a generation that seems to have lost its way, but the authors proceed from their analysis to the practical issues of city planning and offer a strategy of recovery. The authors argue that the story of modern society has been a story of a running battle between the twin elements of modernity – the impulse of individual freedom on the one hand, and the restraints of order and collectivity on the other – and that the process of this battle has not proceeded in a straight line but convulsively, through violent reaction and counter-reaction. Each utopia has been formed on the ruins of the previous one. They argue that we cannot escape from the dissolving forces of today's Postmodern globalism by constructing some new utopian grand narrative. Their prescription is that we work, through an inclusive process, towards Patrick Geddes's ideal of the city as the outcome of a reconciliation of people, places and historical process: that is to say, Geddes's 'Eutopia'. (Geddes, in talking of utopias, pointed out that Sir Thomas More was a shrewd punster. U-topia is not Greek. But Ou-topia means no-place, and so the impossible ideal.) The authors advocate 'planning', therefore, but not planning in the sense in which it was understood in the period that authors label as Modernist. Instead they put forward a cumulative approach to the idea of progress rather than a rejection of the past, and a new phase in the modern search for openness and freedom, offering intimacy by choice, and identity by choice. They seem to be suggesting something like jazz, rather than music played from a score.

The book is not an easy read, but a stimulating one for the reader who perseveres. If you live outside Scotland do not be put off by the focus on Scottish history and geography, because many of the arguments and conclusions apply elsewhere.

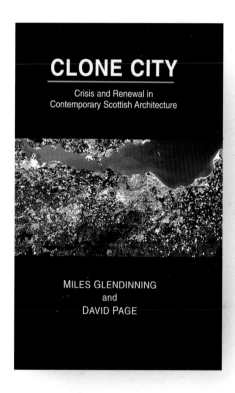

CLONE CITY

Crisis and Renewal in
Contemporary Scottish Architecture

MILES GLENDINNING
and
DAVID PAGE

River and Rowing Museum at Henley-on-Thames

Two years after it was built, David Chipperfield's River and Rowing Museum at Henley has been awarded the Best Building in England 1999 by the Royal Fine Art Commission and British Sky Broadcasting. Helen Castle *went to visit the museum and find out why adulation for this seemingly discreet building only seems to be continuing to grow.*

Like a novel in which the skill and strength of the narrative takes over, overriding any awareness of the author's voice, the River and Rowing Museum stands alone as a building. Its use, programme and site, rather than an architect's signature motifs, are the subject of its architecture. It is no coincidence that most of the descriptions and articles already written about the museum concentrate on its material qualities and context rather than the architect's oeuvre and other architects' work. Discussion of the museum is not dependent on reference to any other building. It is as if, in designing the museum, David Chipperfield was able to cast every architectural assumption aside and start from scratch. Each aspect of the River and Rowing Museum has been ruminated upon and thought afresh. He himself has described the design process as one of 'redescribing in detail'.

Standing in front of the museum for the first time you cannot help being struck by a sense of wonder: how could someone have conceived of such an unlikely blending of parts with such a strong sense of *commoditas*? Raised off the ground on modernist piloti with a concrete deck and a concrete bridge, the museum incorporates an expansive ribbon window which wraps around the main rear facade, but is also clad in silvery weathered, green, oak boards with twin pitched roofs. It is as if heroic Modernism has met with simple rustic vernacular through a process of osmosis – fine detailing and craftsmanship being the unifying forces. The composition is strikingly imaginative, but also entirely fitting to its use and surroundings.

In a location such as Henley-on-Thames commodiousness and a sensitivity to site are a priority. One of the most conservative of historic towns in the Home Coun-

ties, it would have opposed the building of anything less. For most architects the options for the museum would have seemed to have been limited to historical pastiche or a polite contextualism. Terry Farrell, only a few years earlier, responded to a site closer to the centre of the town on the river, with a small building for the Regatta in a heavy rhetorical style.

Chipperfield, however, was able to look beyond the tourist image of the town and strip off the heritage veneer. He looked to the river for his main references: to the boathouses and the marquees erected for Henley Regatta. These provide the external language of the scheme, the long-clad sides of the building and the pitched roofs. He then capitalised on its vicinity to the Thames by placing the building right up to the riverside edge of the large site with a car park behind, so that only Meadow Mill, a small unbuilt-up park, is between the museum and the river. The main or open elevation of the museum is at the rear; the ground floor of the gallery building is glazed with an extensive decked terrace and ramp to the public entrance. Looking back from the towpath to the museum, all that can be seen of the building is a long-clad side framed by a row of poplars. It's a combination which bears all the poetic simplicity of a French pastoral scene.

One of the most extraordinary aspects of the museum is that it was designed before the curators had acquired a collection for it. Rather than being driven by the desire to house specific objects, the project was fuelled by the desire to have a permanent exhibition space for rowing, and subsequently the river. At the 1984 Olympic Games in Los Angeles a temporary rowing exhibition at Santa Barbara inspired a group of British enthusiasts to found their own museum. Henley as the home of the

Regatta was the logical place for it. The lack of an existing collection, however, meant that when fundraising the projected building alone became the main focus for the museum. Commissioned in 1989, construction did not start until 1994.

It seems that with Chipperfield the founders of the museum took a calculated risk. They commissioned a building that would on its own merits draw in visitors, broadening the public appeal for the museum, and enthusing them with their own passion for their sport. This is most apparent in the two parallel, upstairs top-lit galleries, which take the form of upturned hulls with all the finesse of the lightest and most technically advanced crafts. The roof is used to greatest dramatic effect in the room where the racing boats are exhibited by being hung from the ceiling. Another important part of the scheme is the Riverside Café, an attraction in itself – on the road to Henley it is given as much signage as the museum. Wrapped in glass with a handsome floor of polished precast slabs and deep blue and yellow furniture, it has the urbane ambience of a European restaurant or a modern art museum (umbrellas and sculpture on the outside terrace complete this impression).

In his *Theoretical Practice* of 1994, Chipperfield states that it is a lack of time that most often jeopardises architecture. The River and Rowing Museum supports his case. Having taken eight years to build, it exudes the consideration that was bequeathed on it.

From 5 November 1999 – 5 March 2000 a retrospective of David Chipperfield's work, 'Architecture for a New Century', is being shown at the River and Rowing Museum.

Many thanks to Evelyn Stern and Nicole Woodman of David Chipperfield Architects for their help with this article.